MASSACHUSETTS
TRIVIA

MASSACHUSETTS
TRIVIA

COMPILED BY DANIEL & LISA RAMUS

Rutledge Hill Press
NASHVILLE, TENNESSEE

Published by Rutledge Hill Press, Inc., 513 Third Avenue South, Nashville, Tennessee 37210

Typography by Bailey Typography, Inc.
Cover design by Ernie Couch.

Library of Congress Cataloging-in-Publication Data

Ramus, Daniel, 1960-
    Massachusetts trivia / compiled by Daniel and Lisa Ramus.
        p. cm.
    ISBN 1-55853-065-7
    1. Massachusetts—Miscellanea. 2. Questions and answers.
I. Ramus, Lisa, 1958- . II. Title.
F64.5.R36   1990   90-33148
974.4—dc20   CIP

Printed in the United States of America
1 2 3 4 5 6 7 8 — 95 94 93 92 91 90

PREFACE

"The Spirit of Massachusetts
is the Spirit of America"

From its fledgling frontier with Pilgrims and Indians,
through the words of its politicians and writers so
richly reflected in its schools and museums; standing
across its salt sea reaches with cranberries and clam-
bakes, witches and whales . . .

Massachusetts has it all.

Whether you read this book to test your knowledge,
display your erudition, or simply to learn more about
the "Spirit" of essential New England, we hope that
you enjoy the book as much as we have enjoyed pre-
paring it for you.

Good Luck!

—Dan and Lisa Ramus

To the original Pilgrims—
for finding us a home!

TABLE OF CONTENTS

GEOGRAPHY

CHAPTER ONE

Q. What can be found in the canopy above Plymouth Rock?

A. Bones of the Pilgrims.

———◆———

Q. What Massachusetts city holds the country's third largest St. Patrick's Day Parade?

A. Holyoke.

———◆———

Q. In Mendon, where is the largest display of animals in New England?

A. Southwick Wild Animal Farm.

———◆———

Q. To whom does the "Man in the Wheel" monument in Gloucester pay tribute?

A. Brave sea captains.

———◆———

Q. What two towns have ferries to Martha's Vineyard and Nantucket?

A. Hyannis and Woods Hole.

Q. What are the two tallest buildings in Boston?

A. John Hancock Tower and Prudential Tower.

———◆———

Q. How much money is saved by purchasing a bleacher seat at Fenway Park in advance?

A. $1.00.

———◆———

Q. What island off Chatham, Cape Cod, is a National Wildlife Refuge?

A. Monomoy Island.

———◆———

Q. What state road is intersected by Routes 91, 86, 290, 7, and 495?

A. Massachusetts Turnpike.

———◆———

Q. A factory in Orange was the first to manufacture what type of vehicle?

A. Automobile.

———◆———

Q. What fruit grows along the tracks of the Edaville Railroad in South Carver?

A. Cranberries.

———◆———

Q. What is the nickname of the First National Bank of Boston building?

A. The pregnant building.

Q. In what month is New England's Eastern States Exposition held?

A. September.

———◆———

Q. Bartholomew's Cobble has the greatest concentration in the northeast of what plant?

A. Ferns.

———◆———

Q. What does the Nashoba Valley Winery use to make wine instead of grapes?

A. Various fruits.

———◆———

Q. Seventeen villages and neighborhoods, including Woods Hole, make up what Cape Cod town?

A. Falmouth.

———◆———

Q. Other than art and furniture, what is displayed at the Isabella Gardner Museum?

A. Flowers.

———◆———

Q. What town is a two and one-half-hour ferry ride southeast of Hyannis?

A. Nantucket.

———◆———

Q. Because of the concentration of knitting mills in Fall River, what was the city's nickname?

A. The Spindle City.

Q. What is the number of the route called the Boston Post Road?

A. One.

———◆———

Q. For what war is the battleship USS *Massachusetts* the official state memorial?

A. World War II.

———◆———

Q. What is the second largest city in New England?

A. Worcester.

———◆———

Q. Where is Chicama Vineyards, the first winery in Massachusetts?

A. Martha's Vineyard.

———◆———

Q. What highway has been called "America's Technology Highway"?

A. Route 128.

———◆———

Q. In 1602, what island did Bartholomew Gosnold name for the wild grapes and one of his daughters?

A. Martha's Vineyard.

———◆———

Q. What can be seen at Garden in the Woods in Framingham?

A. 1,500 species of wild flowers.

Q. Where is the Boston mayor's office and council chamber?

A. Boston City Hall.

———◆———

Q. Where are fossil tracks of prehistoric animals imbedded in sandstone cliffs?

A. Dinosaur Land.

———◆———

Q. What two bridges cross the Cape Cod Canal?

A. Sagamore and Bourne.

———◆———

Q. How are the swan boats in Boston Public Garden propelled?

A. By foot pedals.

———◆———

Q. What Massachusetts route is also known as "The Great Trail" and "The King's Highway"?

A. 20.

———◆———

Q. The plantings in Mytoi Gardens, on Chappaquiddick Island, are in what ethnic style?

A. Japanese.

———◆———

Q. Where is Tufts New England Medical Center situated?

A. Boston.

Q. What is the largest winery in New England?

A. Commonwealth.

———◆———

Q. What type of tree, growing in Sunderland, is said to be the largest of its kind east of the Mississippi?

A. Sycamore.

———◆———

Q. A round stone barn is a classic example of what kind of architecture?

A. Shaker.

———◆———

Q. What is the oldest restaurant in Boston?

A. Union Oyster House.

———◆———

Q. At Fenway Park, what seats are the most expensive?

A. Field box seats.

———◆———

Q. What body of water covers parts of Dana, Enfield, Greenwich, and Prescott?

A. Quabbin Reservoir.

———◆———

Q. What French phrase was slurred into The Dry Salvages?

A. *Les Trois Sauvages.*

Q. What Boston restaurant has no sign or street number and uses only crumbs on fried food?

A. The No Name Restaurant.

---◆---

Q. In what city does the ferry from Provincetown land during the summer?

A. Boston.

---◆---

Q. What Boston-made ship led the Tall Ships into Boston Harbor in June 1976?

A. The USS *Constitution*.

---◆---

Q. What major road in Boston is crossed by the Arthur Fiedler footbridge?

A. Storrow Drive.

---◆---

Q. What is the name of the pond in Boston Common?

A. Frog Pond.

---◆---

Q. What MBTA line runs from Cambridge to Braintree?

A. Red Line.

---◆---

Q. In what town on Cape Cod do all major roads converge to become one, which then goes to Provincetown?

A. Orleans.

Q. Where in Massachusetts is the Race Point Lighthouse?

A. Provincetown, Cape Cod.

———◆———

Q. How must a camper get to his campsite at the Gillette Castle State Park?

A. By boat.

———◆———

Q. What river flows northeast through Lowell, Lawrence, and Haverhill?

A. Merrimack.

———◆———

Q. What garden is America's first public botanical garden?

A. Boston Public Garden.

———◆———

Q. To what store does the phrase "designer originals from F. B." refer?

A. Filene's Basement.

———◆———

Q. Blackstone Street in Boston is the site of what open air market?

A. Haymarket.

———◆———

Q. What city in the Commonwealth is the birthplace of the U.S. Coast Guard?

A. Newburyport.

Q. What can youth groups do on board the battleship USS *Massachusetts*, in the Fall River?

A. Camp.

———◆———

Q. What is lighted and visible for miles at the Madonna Queen National Shrine in East Boston?

A. A neon cross.

———◆———

Q. What railroad runs from Braintree to Hyannis?

A. Cape Cod and Hyannis Railroad.

———◆———

Q. What beverage is served at the Beaver II in Boston?

A. Revolutionary tea.

———◆———

Q. In what town is Boston Hill situated?

A. North Andover.

———◆———

Q. In Gardner, what oversized replica stands two stories high?

A. A chair.

———◆———

Q. Which Boston tunnel is longer, the Sumner or the Callahan?

A. Sumner.

Q. What Cape Cod public library has an outstanding collection of works dealing with John F. Kennedy?

A. Hyannis Public Library.

———◆———

Q. What New England seashore has one of the last natural beach and sand dune areas on the Atlantic Coast?

A. Cape Cod National Seashore.

———◆———

Q. Plum Island is part of what city?

A. Newburyport.

———◆———

Q. The stone tower in the Mount Auburn Cemetery in Cambridge is a memorial to what president?

A. George Washington.

———◆———

Q. What is the oldest public park in the nation?

A. Boston Common.

———◆———

Q. What two bays are connected by the Cape Cod Canal?

A. Buzzards and Cape Cod.

———◆———

Q. Where is the famous North Bridge?

A. Concord.

Q. What island in Boston Harbor houses the Suffolk County House of Correction?

A. Deer Island.

———◆———

Q. The Cape Cod Melody Tent is in what town?

A. Hyannis.

———◆———

Q. Where is the tallest all-granite monument in the United States?

A. Provincetown (Pilgrim Monument).

———◆———

Q. What city is home to the University of Massachusetts Medical School?

A. Worcester.

———◆———

Q. What north shore beach had a problem with a large deer population?

A. Crane's Beach.

———◆———

Q. What is the route number of the Massachusetts Turnpike?

A. 90.

———◆———

Q. Martha's Vineyard is in what county?

A. Dukes.

Q. Route 28 is on what side of Cape Cod?

A. Southern.

Q. What Boston structure is home to the Ancient and Honorable Artillery Company?

A. Faneuil Hall.

Q. What town is home to the largest lobster distributor in America?

A. Gloucester.

Q. What collapsed the "Where's Boston?" exhibit when it was at the Prudential Center in Boston?

A. Blizzard of 1978.

Q. The Mohawk Trail, a 63-mile Indian trail in western Massachusetts, is now what route?

A. Two.

Q. The oldest and largest United States celebration of what nationality takes place annually in New Bedford?

A. Portuguese.

Q. Is the toll for Boston's Mystic Tobin Bridge charged for going into Boston, out of Boston, or both ways?

A. Going into Boston.

Q. What is the largest military installation in New England?

A. Fort Devens.

———◆———

Q. What insect's statue is on top of Faneuil Hall?

A. A grasshopper.

———◆———

Q. What can be seen at the finale of the Boston Pops' Fourth of July concert?

A. Fireworks.

———◆———

Q. Boston Lighthouse, the first lighthouse in America, is on what island?

A. Little Brewster.

———◆———

Q. On what hill is the Boston State House built?

A. Beacon.

———◆———

Q. What New England fair is called the "Big E"?

A. Eastern States Exposition.

———◆———

Q. What is the only state park in Massachusetts that requires overnight reservations?

A. Boston Harbor Islands.

Q. On what island are half a million lobsters hatched annually at the Massachusetts State Lobster Hatchery?

A. Martha's Vineyard.

Q. What town is depicted in Norman Mailer's book *Tough Guys Don't Dance*?

A. Provincetown.

Q. What type of footbridge is in the Boston Public Garden?

A. Suspension.

Q. What is the nickname of the USS *Massachusetts*, situated in Fall River?

A. "Big Mamie."

Q. What MBTA line has a stop at Symphony Hall?

A. Green Line.

Q. What town is a 45-minute ferry ride south from Woods Hole?

A. Martha's Vineyard.

Q. Where are Gay Head Cliffs, Lighthouse Beach, and Oak Bluffs Beach?

A. Martha's Vineyard.

Q. The Natural Bridge, situated in North Adams, is made up of what material?

A. Marble.

———◆———

Q. What bay is crossed by the ferry from New Bedford to Martha's Vineyard?

A. Buzzards.

———◆———

Q. What society manages and maintains a 43-acre garden in the woods in Framingham?

A. New England Wild Flower Society.

———◆———

Q. What maritime school is situated on Buzzards Bay?

A. Massachusetts Maritime Academy.

———◆———

Q. What subway station is outside the entrance to the Boston Garden?

A. North Station.

———◆———

Q. What trail did the Indians of the Five Nations use to pass between the Connecticut Valley and the Hudson Valley?

A. Mohawk Trail.

———◆———

Q. What peninsula was named by Bartholomew Gosnold in 1602?

A. Cape Cod.

Q. How many twentieth-century United States navy fighting ships are displayed at Battleship Cove?

A. Five.

———◆———

Q. What is the only national seashore in New England?

A. Cape Cod.

———◆———

Q. What town was named for its English counterpart?

A. Framingham.

———◆———

Q. What kind of stone was used to build the west wing of the Museum of Fine Arts in Boston?

A. Granite.

———◆———

Q. What company makes glass in Sandwich?

A. Sandwich Glass Company.

———◆———

Q. Where is the New England Aquarium?

A. Boston.

———◆———

Q. What is the oldest town on Cape Cod?

A. Sandwich.

Q. What ship is found at the state pier in Plymouth?

A. *Mayflower II.*

Q. What Manchester beach was named for the sound the sand makes when walked on?

A. Singing Beach.

———◆———

Q. The Forbes Public Library in Northampton has a collection of the papers of what United States president?

A. Calvin Coolidge.

———◆———

Q. In what town is the Kennedy family compound situated?

A. Hyannisport.

———◆———

Q. What is the toll on the Massachusetts Turnpike between routes 290 and 84?

A. 40 cents.

———◆———

Q. On what floor is the John Hancock building observatory?

A. 60.

———◆———

Q. What town is at the tip of Cape Cod?

A. Provincetown.

Q. Where are Children's Beach, Brant Point, and Cisco Beach?

A. Nantucket Island.

Q. What university is in Medford?

A. Tufts.

Q. What four towns make up the Cape Ann area?

A. Rockport, Gloucester, Essex, and Manchester.

Q. Shortly after it was built, what Boston skyscraper had problems with the windows popping out?

A. John Hancock Tower.

Q. On what days is Boston's Haymarket shopping area open for the sale of produce?

A. Friday and Saturday.

Q. How are the grounds of children's author Thornton Burgess's home now used?

A. Massachusetts Audubon Society Wildlife Sanctuary.

Q. What Faneuil Hall market stocks the largest variety of food?

A. Quincy.

Q. Where is a collection of glass flowers that attracts more than 180,000 viewers each year?

A. Botanical Museum of Harvard University.

———◆———

Q. What are the four colors of the subway lines in Boston?

A. Orange, blue, red, and green.

———◆———

Q. Which island is larger, Martha's Vineyard or Nantucket?

A. Martha's Vineyard.

———◆———

Q. Where does the Freedom Trail begin?

A. Boston Common.

———◆———

Q. Of what material is the "Paper House" in Pigeon Cove constructed?

A. Newspapers (about 100,000 of them).

———◆———

Q. In what square are Quincy Market and Faneuil Hall found?

A. Dock Square.

———◆———

Q. What town was named after William Pitt?

A. Pittsfield.

Q. What city is the geographic center of Massachusetts?

A. Worcester.

Q. What color is the New England Aquarium building?

A. Gray.

Q. What is the full-length toll for a car on the Massachusetts Turnpike?

A. $4.30.

Q. The life-size statue of astronomer Dr. Nathaniel Bowditch in Cambridge was the first of its kind to be made of what material?

A. Bronze.

Q. The largest turtle shell ever found is at what University's museum?

A. Harvard.

Q. What revitalized wharf, complete with shops and restaurants, is in Salem?

A. Pickering.

Q. By what name is Route 30 known in Boston?

A. Commonwealth Avenue.

Q. How long is Boston's Freedom Trail?

A. One-and-one-half miles.

————◆————

Q. How many beaches on the Cape Cod National Seashore are manned by lifeguards?

A. Six.

————◆————

Q. What man's Boston statue has four bronze panels, one of which depicts experiments with lighting?

A. Benjamin Franklin.

————◆————

Q. Why is the town of Norwell unique?

A. It is the only town in the United States with that name.

————◆————

Q. What river flows through Boston?

A. Charles.

————◆————

Q. What manmade lake is the largest in the northeast?

A. Quabbin Reservoir.

————◆————

Q. What island is often called "The Gray Lady"?

A. Nantucket.

Q. Why is Massachusetts called the Bay State?

A. In reference to Cape Cod Bay.

Q. What percentage of today's downtown Boston is man-made land?

A. 60 percent.

Q. What county has 300 miles of shoreline?

A. Barnstable (Cape Cod).

Q. What is the highest peak in Massachusetts?

A. Mount Greylock (3,491 feet).

Q. What is the longest river situated entirely within Massachusetts?

A. Charles.

Q. In what harbor are Grape and Bumpkin islands situated?

A. Boston.

Q. The First Unitarian Church of Christ in Lancaster was designed by what famous architect?

A. Charles Bulfinch.

Q. How much would the summer ferry cost, round trip from Hyannis to Nantucket, for a car and driver?

A. $150.00.

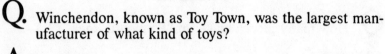

Q. Winchendon, known as Toy Town, was the largest manufacturer of what kind of toys?

A. Wooden.

Q. What makes East Boston's Constitution Beach so noisy?

A. Logan Airport air traffic.

Q. What is the biggest industry on Cape Cod today?

A. Tourism.

Q. What city's motto is "God be with us as he was with our fathers"?

A. Boston.

Q. What Hyannis candle factory is the largest?

A. Colonial Candle of Cape Cod.

Q. In 1984, what Massachusetts crime rate ranking did Marlborough receive?

A. Lowest in the state.

Q. In 1960, Massachusetts had the largest percentage of foreign-born residents in the United States, except for what state?

A. New York.

———◆———

Q. How many pieces make up "Plymouth Rock"?

A. Two.

———◆———

Q. What Hebrew word was first given as the name of Salem?

A. *Shalom.*

———◆———

Q. Who is the Mystic Tobin Bridge named after?

A. Maurice J. Tobin.

———◆———

Q. What road was named for John F. Kennedy's maternal grandfather?

A. John F. Fitzgerald Expressway.

———◆———

Q. At the last census, how many American Indians and Eskimos were part of Boston's 562,994 residents?

A. 1,455.

———◆———

Q. What national background is prevalent in the "North End" of Boston?

A. Italian.

Q. What is the largest commercial port in New England?

A. Port of Boston.

Q. What airport has the world's tallest airport tower?

A. Logan.

Q. Where are John Hancock, Samuel Adams, and Paul Revere buried?

A. Old Granary burying grounds.

Q. The National Historical Park in Lowell commemorates what revolution?

A. Industrial Revolution.

Q. Approximately how many miles is it from Boston to Providence, Rhode Island?

A. 46.

Q. What organization, known as the AYH, is a world-wide organization with offices in Massachusetts?

A. American Youth Hostels.

Q. How long is the ferry ride from Boston to Provincetown?

A. Three hours.

Q. On a clear day, what three states can be seen from Pigeon Hill on Cape Ann?

A. Massachusetts, New Hampshire, and Maine.

———◆———

Q. How many buildings in New England are more than sixty stories high?

A. None.

———◆———

Q. The Merrimack River originates on the western slopes of the White Mountains and flows to what port city?

A. Newburyport.

———◆———

Q. What is the meaning of the pineapple symbol found at many Massachusetts bed-and-breakfast establishments?

A. Hospitality.

———◆———

Q. What major highway goes through Connecticut, Massachusetts, and Vermont?

A. Route 91.

———◆———

Q. Approximately how many miles is it from Hyannis to Hartford, Connecticut?

A. 136.

———◆———

Q. What do the initials stand for in B & M Railroad?

A. Boston and Maine.

Q. What two New England states observe April 16th (Patriots' Day) as a state holiday?

A. Massachusetts and Maine.

———◆———

Q. According to the 1980 census, how are the New England states ranked, from the largest population to the smallest?

A. Massachusetts, Connecticut, Maine, Rhode Island, New Hampshire, and Vermont.

———◆———

Q. How many counties are in Massachusetts?

A. 14.

———◆———

Q. Where is the Boston police headquarters?

A. Berkley Street.

———◆———

Q. Where is the famed Bay Tower Room in Boston?

A. 60 State Street.

———◆———

Q. Where is the largest clock in Boston?

A. Customs House.

———◆———

Q. Where can Boston visitors climb in Grandma's Attic and work on an assembly line?

A. Children's Museum.

Q. What is Boston's sister city?

A. Kyoto, Japan.

———◆———

Q. Where is the Peabody Museum?

A. Salem.

———◆———

Q. What color is the line on the sidewalk that traces the Freedom Trail?

A. Red.

———◆———

Q. What signal is given by Minot's Light off Cohasset?

A. "I love you."

———◆———

Q. How many main buildings does Faneuil Hall have?

A. Three.

———◆———

Q. What religious order runs St. Joseph Abbey in Spencer?

A. Trappist.

———◆———

Q. What town boasts the John Alden House, the furnished home of the *Mayflower* emigres?

A. Duxbury.

Q. The Old Derby Academy in Hingham was the first United States school of what type?

A. Co-educational.

Q. In Middleboro, this "Village" houses over 2,000 international models of what type?

A. Trains.

Q. During what year was Plimoth Plantation settled?

A. 1620.

Q. In what town can visitors take a 5½-mile train ride through 1,800 acres of cranberry bogs?

A. South Carver.

Q. A former U.S. Coast Guard Station in Hull now houses what museum?

A. Hull Lifesaving Museum.

Q. The whaler *Acushnet* was fitted out in what town?

A. Fairhaven.

Q. During the nineteenth century, Fall River was the world capital of what type of manufacturing?

A. Cotton textile.

Q. An original edition of *Moby Dick,* situated in New Bedford, is bound with the hide of what animal?

A. Porpoise.

———◆———

Q. Hundreds of shipwrecks occurred near what town, known as Cape Cod's "elbow"?

A. Chatham.

———◆———

Q. What is special about the organ at the Congregational Church in Dennis?

A. It is the oldest working organ in the country.

———◆———

Q. What will visitors find at the Ashumet Holly Reservation in East Falmouth?

A. Forty acres of holly plantings and shrubs.

———◆———

Q. Where is the Drummer Boy Museum?
A. Brewster.

———◆———

Q. First Encounter Beach in Eastham was the site of a battle between what two groups?

A. Indians and Pilgrims.

———◆———

Q. The Congregational Church in Falmouth contains a bell made by what famous patriot?

A. Paul Revere.

Q. What famous Norse explorer is commemorated by a statue on Commonwealth Avenue in Boston?

A. Leif Ericson.

Q. Of the 23 "witches" executed in 1692, 12 were from what town?

A. Danvers.

Q. The town clock in Wellfleet strikes what kind of time?

A. Ship's time (1 to 8 bells).

Q. What is the Victorian-style town on Martha's Vineyard?

A. Oak Bluffs.

Q. Where is the "Art Capital" of Cape Cod?

A. Provincetown.

Q. What did Thomas Mayhew pay for Nantucket?

A. 30 (English) pounds and 2 beaver hats.

Q. On what island can visitors see a whale skeleton?

A. Nantucket.

Q. Where is the John F. Kennedy Library and Museum?

A. Dorchester.

———◆———

Q. In what town was John F. Kennedy born?

A. Brookline.

———◆———

Q. Where is the Minuteman National Historic Park?

A. Concord.

———◆———

Q. What famous cemetery contains the graves of Emerson, Thoreau, Alcott, and Hawthorne?

A. Sleepy Hollow Cemetery.

———◆———

Q. What state forest is in South Carver?

A. Miles Standish.

———◆———

Q. Where is the Forefathers Monument, the largest granite monument of its kind?

A. Plymouth.

———◆———

Q. Designed by Frederick Law Olmsted, what reservation in located in Hingham?

A. World's End.

Q. Harwich is Cape Cod's leading producer of what fruit?

A. Cranberry.

———◆———

Q. What is the more common name of the Highland Light in North Truro, one of the most powerful lights on the Atlantic Coast?

A. Cape Cod Light.

———◆———

Q. What is the translation of Lake Chargoggagoggman-chauggaggoggchaubunagungamaugg (Lake Webster)?

A. "I fish on my side of the lake, you fish on yours and no one fishes in between."

———◆———

Q. In what state park in Hadley is hang gliding a popular sport?

A. Skinner.

———◆———

Q. Where is the home of the Pioneer Valley Symphony?

A. Greenfield.

———◆———

Q. What kind of footprints are located in Granby?

A. Dinosaur tracks.

———◆———

Q. What town hosts the Berkshire Balloon Festival?

A. Cummington.

Q. What does *Agawam* mean in the Indian language?

A. "Crooked river."

———◆———

Q. Where does the Mid-State Trail begin?

A. Mount Watatic.

———◆———

Q. Where is the Wisteriahurst Fine Arts Museum?

A. Holyoke.

———◆———

Q. The Sophia Smith Collection in Northampton is home to more than 500,000 papers on what subject?

A. The social and intellectual history of women.

———◆———

Q. What famous trail opened in Orange in 1914?

A. Mohawk.

———◆———

Q. What town is home to the first (1960) atomic energy plant in New England?

A. Rowe.

———◆———

Q. Where is the site of the first navigable canal in the United States, built in 1795 on the Connecticut River?

A. South Hadley.

Q. What city was founded by William Pynchon in 1636?

A. Springfield.

Q. What village is the highest on the Mohawk Trail?

A. Florida.

Q. What novelist lived at "The Mount" in Lenox?

A. Edith Wharton.

Q. What Wellesley college houses a 28-foot steel globe of the world?

A. Babson College.

Q. How tall is Mount Wachusett in Princeton?

A. 2,006 feet.

Q. How many four-year colleges are situated in Worcester?

A. Seven.

Q. What river plunges through the gorge in West Chester-field?

A. Westfield.

Q. Why is 70 percent of the land in Truro protected from development?

A. It is within the Cape Cod National Seashore.

———◆———

Q. What Cape Cod town is known as "the first stop of the east wind"?

A. Chatham.

———◆———

Q. Steep Hill Beach is in what town?

A. Ipswich.

———◆———

Q. What major route runs through Sheffield, Stockbridge, and Lenox?

A. Seven.

———◆———

Q. What route is the only major road running to Provincetown?

A. Six.

———◆———

Q. What is the last town on the northernmost point of Route 128?

A. Gloucester.

———◆———

Q. What building now occupies the site of the former federal reserve bank in Boston?

A. A French hotel.

Q. What town is known as the "Queen of the mill towns"?

A. Lawrence.

———◆———

Q. What is the Seaman's Bethel, situated in New Bedford?

A. A chapel.

———◆———

Q. Where is the Commonwealth Winery?

A. Plymouth.

———◆———

Q. On what street is the Guild of Boston Artists?

A. Newbury.

———◆———

Q. Where is Sullivan Stadium?

A. Foxboro.

———◆———

Q. How much is the fare on the Water Taxi in the Boston Islands State Park?

A. It is free.

———◆———

Q. In what year was the Granite Railway in Quincy, the first commercial railroad in the United States, built?

A. 1826.

Q. The first large ironworks in the Colonies was in what town?

A. Saugus.

———◆———

Q. What hill in Sharon is the oldest Audubon Sanctuary in Massachusetts?

A. Moose Hill.

———◆———

Q. What town is the site of the first 4-arch stone bridge?

A. Sudbury.

———◆———

Q. Minutemen gathered at what famous Lexington tavern before the April 15, 1775, battle with the British?

A. Buckman.

———◆———

Q. Where is the Charles River Museum of Industry?

A. Waltham.

———◆———

Q. The Cardinal Spellman Philatelic Museum in Weston has over 300,000 international examples of what collectible?

A. Stamps.

———◆———

Q. Where is the birthplace of Abigail Adams?

A. North Weymouth.

ENTERTAINMENT

C H A P T E R   T W O

Q. In what quaint downtown area was *The Witches of East-wick* filmed?

A. Cohasset.

———◆———

Q. What television station did the Boston Celtics purchase?

A. Fox station 25.

———◆———

Q. What husband and wife team anchor the News at 6 on ABC?

A. Natalie Jacobson and Chet Curtis.

———◆———

Q. Who is the resident doctor for ABC News and "Good Morning, America"?

A. Dr. Timothy Johnson.

———◆———

Q. What show features "Main Streets and Backroads of New England"?

A. "Chronicle."

Q. For what newspaper does Mike Barnacle regularly write?

A. *Boston Globe.*

Q. Dave Murry, weatherman for NBC 6 O'clock News, came from what morning television show?

A. "Good Morning, America."

Q. Where is the Great Woods Center for the Performing Arts?

A. Mansfield.

Q. What kind of programming is on Boston's WBCN–FM at 5:05 P.M.?

A. Comedy.

Q. Where is the South Shore Music Circus?

A. Cohasset.

Q. What suspense-filled play is the longest running show in Boston?

A. *Shear Madness.*

Q. What bridge is crossed by visitors to the Boston Tea Party Ship and Museum?

A. Congress Street Bridge.

Q. On what major television station does Liz Walker co-anchor the news?

A. NBC.

———◆———

Q. Dave Maynard hosts what radio station's morning show?

A. WBZ.

———◆———

Q. What celebrity hosts "Talent Showcase"?

A. Dave Maynard.

———◆———

Q. What radio station sponsors the "Rock of Boston" concert?

A. WBCN.

———◆———

Q. Who is Charles Laquidara?

A. A WBCN radio morning host.

———◆———

Q. What is the oldest shopping mall east of the Mississippi?

A. Shoppers World, Framingham.

———◆———

Q. In the art world, for what do the letters I. C. A. stand?

A. Institute of Contemporary Art.

Q. What kind of business is Shreve, Crump and Low on Boylston Street in Boston?

A. Jewelry store.

————◆————

Q. What type of shirt did John F. Kennedy dislike, urging his staff not to wear them?

A. Shirts with button-down collars.

————◆————

Q. Why did one Brinks robbery gang member complain to the police?

A. He did not receive his share of the money.

————◆————

Q. What kind of specialty food does the Magic Pan restaurant in Boston serve?

A. Crepes.

————◆————

Q. On a per capita basis, what is stolen more often in Massachusetts than in any other state in the union?

A. Cars.

————◆————

Q. What Boston band recorded the song "Freeze-Frame"?

A. The J. Geils Band.

————◆————

Q. Written in Massachusetts, "My Country 'Tis of Thee" is another name for what song?

A. "America."

Q. What game has been produced by Parker Brothers in Massachusetts for nearly fifty years?

A. Monopoly.

Q. What cookie was named after Newton?

A. The fig newton.

Q. In 1953, what did Bette Davis have surgically removed?

A. Half her jaw.

Q. Arthur Fiedler did a commercial for what liquor?

A. Black and White Scotch.

Q. Inspector Faraday was the policeman in what radio and television series?

A. "Boston Blackie."

Q. At the Fourth of July Esplanade Concert in Boston, what song is usually played last?

A. "Stars and Stripes Forever."

Q. In what part of the Newton-Wellesley Hospital was Jack Lemmon born?

A. An elevator.

Q. What "all-day sucker" was developed by the Bradley-Smith Candy Company?

A. Lollipop.

---◆---

Q. The Cabot Street Cinema Theatre in Beverly is famous for what type of entertainment?

A. Magic shows.

---◆---

Q. What products can visitors learn about at the John H. Breck Company in Springfield?

A. Hair-care products.

---◆---

Q. What has been made at Walter Baker and Company in Dorchester since 1765?

A. Chocolate.

---◆---

Q. What children's television show, filmed in Boston, featured insects called the "Do Bee" and the "Don't Bee"?

A. "Romper Room."

---◆---

Q. What "M*A*S*H" character was from Boston?

A. Major Charles Emerson Winchester, III.

---◆---

Q. What rock group was bailed out of jail by Major Kevin White so that they could play at the Boston Garden?

A. The Rolling Stones.

Q. What company is the largest employer in the greater Boston area?

A. Raytheon.

———◆———

Q. How many sides does the face of a Susan B. Anthony coin have?

A. 11.

———◆———

Q. What kind of ride is the Cyclone at Riverside Park?

A. Roller coaster.

———◆———

Q. Where was Marshall Field, who founded his store chain in Chicago, born?

A. Conway.

———◆———

Q. According to the song, who could not get off of the "M. T. A."?

A. Charlie.

———◆———

Q. Arlington-born Samuel Wilson is often considered to be the prototype for what patriotic character?

A. Uncle Sam.

———◆———

Q. What brand of pen is made by Gillette?

A. Paper-Mate.

Q. What does Ye Olde Pepper Company of Salem, the oldest company of its kind in America, produce?

A. Candy.

———◆———

Q. When Boston baked beans are made, what are the three most common sweeteners?

A. Brown sugar, molasses, and maple syrup.

———◆———

Q. What is the number of the channel for television station WGBH in Boston?

A. Two.

———◆———

Q. How much money was offered to Boston-born Barbara Walters to pose in Hustler magazine?

A. $1,000,000.

———◆———

Q. A student at what Massachusetts college was crowned Miss New York State in 1985?

A. Pine Manor.

———◆———

Q. What Boston television channel uses the Roman numerals of its number as the last three letters of its call sign?

A. WLVI, Channel 56.

———◆———

Q. What company has the largest pasta-making factory in the United States?

A. Prince Company.

Q. What was Barbara Walters' role on her first television appearance?

A. Model.

———◆———

Q. What figure is the weathervane on top of Quincy Market?

A. A bull.

———◆———

Q. What type of cuisine does Boston's Benihana's restaurant serve?

A. Japanese.

———◆———

Q. What company makes Right Guard deodorant?

A. Gillette.

———◆———

Q. What city was once known as the "Athens of America" because of its wealth?

A. Boston.

———◆———

Q. In 1716, where was the first lion exhibited in America?

A. Boston.

———◆———

Q. What religious sect produced the famous oval finger boxes?

A. The Shakers.

Q. How are Sturbridge Village lawns kept trimmed?

A. With sheep.

———◆———

Q. What is the Massachusetts state beverage?

A. Cranberry juice.

———◆———

Q. Where was Milton Berle first publicly called "Uncle Milty"?

A. On Boston's Boylston Street.

———◆———

Q. In Boston and Suffolk County, what holiday other than St. Patrick's Day is celebrated on March 17?

A. Evacuation Day.

———◆———

Q. Paper patterns were first manufactured in 1863 in Sterling for what company?

A. E. Butterick.

———◆———

Q. What children's television show was hosted by Miss Jean and her magic mirror?

A. "Romper Room."

———◆———

Q. On what currency is Benjamin Franklin's portrait shown?

A. $100 bill.

Q. What kind of greeting card did Louis Prang of Boston print for the first time in America?

A. Christmas card.

———◆———

Q. What radio station broadcasts the Boston Symphony Orchestra from Tanglewood?

A. WGBH, 89.7 FM.

———◆———

Q. What company in Marlborough produces all natural popcorn?

A. Smartfoods Company.

———◆———

Q. What is the married name of Jacqueline Kennedy Onassis' mother?

A. Auchincloss.

———◆———

Q. What radio station broadcasts Boston Celtics games?

A. WEEI–AM, Boston.

———◆———

Q. At what stadium was Michael Jackson refused a permit to perform?

A. Sullivan.

———◆———

Q. What ice cream company has been in business for more than 75 years?

A. Brigham's.

Q. What brewery is on Boston's Portland Street?

A. Commonwealth.

◆

Q. What Wenham company is most famous for its Camembert?

A. Craigston Cheese Company.

◆

Q. What pasta company is situated in Chelsea?

A. Trio's Original Italian Pasta.

◆

Q. During what month is the Daffodil Festival held on Nantucket?

A. April.

◆

Q. Boston Harbor Fest is held during what month?

A. July.

◆

Q. What kind of bread was created to serve with Boston baked beans?

A. Boston brown bread.

◆

Q. What two New England states have the lowest state gas tax per gallon?

A. Massachusetts and Vermont.

Q. What kind of cake is usually served at a Massachusetts strawberry festival?

A. Shortcake.

———◆———

Q. What are "puddings in the belly," served at the first Thanksgiving, now called?

A. Stuffing.

———◆———

Q. What dish was developed because of Puritan restrictions on work on the Sabbath?

A. Baked beans.

———◆———

Q. What three basic items are needed at a typical Cape Cod beach clambake?

A. Hot stones, clams, and a covering of seaweed.

———◆———

Q. What three New England states form an official viti-cultural area?

A. Massachusetts, Connecticut, and Rhode Island.

———◆———

Q. The Harvard student group known as the Pierian Sodality in 1908 is now called by what name?

A. Harvard University Orchestra.

———◆———

Q. Who said, "You're going to have a wedding whether you like it or not" to Debbie Reynolds in *The Catered Affair*?

A. Bette Davis.

Q. What Boston-born singer was originally known as LaDonna Gaines?

A. Donna Summer.

Q. What Boston-born actress made her 1932 film debut in *Murders in the Rue Morgue?*

A. Arlene Francis.

Q. Whose name did Warner Brothers want to change to Bettina Dawes?

A. Bette Davis.

Q. What organization, owner of a famous Boston building, is known by the initials OCB?

A. The Opera Company of Boston.

Q. What orchestra does John Williams conduct?

A. The Boston Pops.

Q. What Boston musical organization celebrated its centennial season in 1985?

A. The Boston Pops.

Q. What infamous Boston criminal did Tony Curtis portray?

A. The Boston Strangler.

Q. What major dance group was founded in 1964?

A. The Boston Ballet.

———◆———

Q. What rock and roll group was voted the Best New Group in 1977 by the Rock Music Association?

A. Boston.

———◆———

Q. What Lawrence-born man is the conductor of the New York Philharmonic?

A. Leonard Bernstein.

———◆———

Q. Who signed off his Boston-filmed television show with "Always keep laughing"?

A. Bozo the Clown.

———◆———

Q. In the movie *Moby Dick,* what actor said, "Aye, it was Moby Dick that tore my soul and body until they bled into each other"?

A. Gregory Peck.

———◆———

Q. What regional television program features the song "Star of the Day, Who Will It Be"?

A. "Community Auditions."

———◆———

Q. For what movie did Bette Davis receive her first Academy Award?

A. *Dangerous* (1935).

Q. Who wrote the official state folk song, "Massachusetts"?

A. Arlo Guthrie.

———◆———

Q. On what Boston-based public television program is home renovation demonstrated?

A. "This Old House."

———◆———

Q. Whose story is presented in *The Miracle Worker?*

A. Helen Keller's.

———◆———

Q. What does Boston's Channel 2 (public television) broadcast several times each year to raise money to support itself?

A. An auction.

———◆———

Q. What was the name of Milton Bradley's first game?

A. Checkered Game of Life.

———◆———

Q. The patron saint of fishing boats is honored by what Gloucester festival?

A. St. Peter's Fiesta.

———◆———

Q. What did Henry Lee Gigginson found and finance in 1881 to enrich society?

A. The Boston Symphony Orchestra.

Q. Who composed the movie score for *Star Wars*?

A. John Williams.

———◆———

Q. From what college did Ali McGraw graduate?

A. Wellesley.

———◆———

Q. Gary Burton, Al DiMeola, and Quincy Jones are a few of the talented graduates of what college?

A. Berklee College of Music.

———◆———

Q. What type of television show was the first interrupted to notify Americans that President Kennedy had been shot?

A. A soap opera.

———◆———

Q. Barry Buller was wearing a Boston University sweatshirt in what science fiction film?

A. *Close Encounters of the Third Kind.*

———◆———

Q. What actor starred in *The Brink's Job,* filmed in Boston?

A. Peter Falk.

———◆———

Q. Boston-born Arlene Kazajian had what name professionally?

A. Arlene Francis.

Q. What former member of the rock group Van Halen grew up in Roxbury?

A. David Lee Roth.

———◆———

Q. On what Boston-based children's television show did the host conclude with "I'll be blasting you"?

A. "Major Mudd."

———◆———

Q. What Martha's Vineyard carnival ride is reputed to be the oldest in America?

A. A carousel.

———◆———

Q. Where is "*Yankee* Magazine's Great New England Cook-Off and Food Festival" held?

A. Faneuil Hall Marketplace, Boston.

———◆———

Q. Where in Boston are half-price theater and concert tickets available on the day of the show?

A. Bostix.

———◆———

Q. In what town is one of the best magic shows in the world held?

A. Beverly.

———◆———

Q. How many days does the Eastern States Exposition run?

A. 12.

Q. What kind of music is played at Boston's Black Rose Restaurant and Bar?

A. Irish.

———◆———

Q. What Springfield fair is the eighth largest in the United States?

A. The Eastern States Exposition.

———◆———

Q. On what street is the John F. Kennedy School of Government situated?

A. John F. Kennedy Street.

———◆———

Q. Brimfield is the home of what thrice-yearly, 1,500-dealer event?

A. Brimfield Flea Market.

———◆———

Q. What Hull amusement park is now a condominium building site?

A. Paragon Park.

———◆———

Q. What Boston bar is the basis for the television show "Cheers"?

A. Bullfinch Pub.

———◆———

Q. What museum houses the "OMNIMAX" theater?

A. Boston Museum of Science.

Q. What performing arts center is in Lenox?

A. Tanglewood.

———◆———

Q. What Boston music group plays in the Esplanade concert on the Fourth of July?

A. The Boston Pops.

———◆———

Q. What is the largest amusement park in New England?

A. Riverside Park, Agawam.

———◆———

Q. Mrs. John F. Kennedy gave the American people a television tour of what building?

A. The White House.

———◆———

Q. What does a gaffer do in a Cape Cod glassmaking establishment?

A. Blows glass.

———◆———

Q. Tom Scholz is the lead guitarist and song writer for what band?

A. Boston.

———◆———

Q. Eileen Prose is the host of what local morning show?

A. "Good Day."

Q. Pianist Seth Justman played for what band?

A. The J. Geils Band.

———◆———

Q. Where is the Remis Auditorium?

A. Museum of Fine Arts.

———◆———

Q. Where is the second oldest canal system in America?

A. Lowell.

———◆———

Q. How many steps and ladders does a visitor have to climb in order to reach the top of the Boston Light House?

A. 76 steps and 2 ladders.

———◆———

Q. The Fairgrounds on Route 1 is the site of what autumn fair?

A. Topsfield.

———◆———

Q. Columbia Point is the location of what famous library?

A. The John F. Kennedy Library.

———◆———

Q. What Boston street is home to the Wilbur and Wang theaters?

A. Tremont.

Q. At what theater is *Shear Madness* performed?

A. Charles Playhouse.

———◆———

Q. On what street is Symphony Hall?

A. Massachusetts Avenue.

———◆———

Q. Where are Arthur Fiedler's baton, Fred Astaire's dancing shoes, and Bette Davis's cookbook?

A. The Special Collections Repository at Boston University.

———◆———

Q. On what Boston wharf is the Computer Museum and the Children's Museum?

A. Museum Wharf.

———◆———

Q. What university houses the Fogg Art Museum?

A. Harvard.

———◆———

Q. What Worcester radio station is 107.3 FM?

A. WAAF.

———◆———

Q. What city is the home of Channel 27, WHLL?

A. Worcester.

Q. At what hotel did the Rolling Stones stay in 1989?

A. The Four Seasons.

Q. For what Boston radio station does Larry Glick work?

A. WHDH.

Q. What Matthew Broderick film was shot in Ipswich?

A. *Glory.*

Q. What was the name of the 1989 Rolling Stones tour?

A. The Steel Wheels Tour.

Q. The Armand LaMontagne sculptures of Bobby Orr and Larry Bird are at what museum?

A. The Sports Museum.

Q. What is "Albert's Almanac"?

A. A weather quiz on Channel 5, on the 6:00 P.M. weekday news.

Q. What university did Tracy Chapman attend?

A. Tufts.

Q. On what Boston street is The Paradise rock club?

A. Commonwealth Avenue.

———◆———

Q. For what do the call letters of WCRB 102.5 FM stand?

A. "We're Classical Radio Boston."

———◆———

Q. What Necco Street nightclub claims to have "Boston's best live rock"?

A. The Channel.

———◆———

Q. Who co-hosts Celtics games on Boston's WEEI–AM with Glen Ordway?

A. Johnny Most.

———◆———

Q. What is the Renaissance marketplace fair held every fall in South Carver?

A. King Richard's Faire.

———◆———

Q. Information on what event can be obtained by calling 413–737–BIGE?

A. The Eastern State Exposition.

———◆———

Q. In what month is the annual Kielbasa Festival held in western Massachusetts?

A. September.

HISTORY

CHAPTER THREE

Q. What metal did Salisbury women melt down to make bullets for the Revolutionary War?

A. Pewter.

———◆———

Q. Former Massachusetts governor Elbridge Gerry was also vice president under what United States president?

A. James Madison.

———◆———

Q. What did a busboy accidentally set on fire while lighting a match to fix a light at the Coconut Grove?

A. A palm tree.

———◆———

Q. From what college did Charles Pillsbury graduate in 1863?

A. Dartmouth.

———◆———

Q. By what nickname is the USS *Constitution* known?

A. "Old Ironsides."

Q. What was the name of the first successful newspaper in America?

A. *Boston News-Letter.*

Q. On what river did Henry David Thoreau sail a home-made scow in 1839?

A. Merrimack.

Q. Who was governor of Plimoth Plantation 31 times?

A. William Bradford.

Q. What trials did Cotton Mather write about in *Warders of the Invisible World?*

A. The Salem witch trials.

Q. What ultraconservative organization was founded in 1958 by Robert Welch, Jr., a retired Boston candy manufacturer?

A. The John Birch Society.

Q. From what English town did the Pilgrims depart?

A. Scrooby.

Q. What two former United States presidents died on the same day?

A. John Adams and Thomas Jefferson (July 4, 1826).

Q. The first white child born in New England was the daughter of what Pilgrim couple?

A. John and Priscilla Alden.

———◆———

Q. What captain led the expedition from Plymouth waters to the shore on December 20, 1620?

A. Miles Standish.

———◆———

Q. What Boston building is known as the Temple of Liberty?

A. Old State House.

———◆———

Q. What name was given to the first U.S. Coast Guard cutter, built in Newburyport?

A. *Massachusetts.*

———◆———

Q. How did the patriots dress for the Boston Tea Party?

A. As Indians.

———◆———

Q. Where were the lanterns hung that signaled "one if by land, two if by sea"?

A. Old North Church.

———◆———

Q. With Massachusetts, what three New England states were part of the original thirteen?

A. Connecticut, New Hampshire, and Rhode Island.

Q. The first Pilgrim settlement was named after what English town?

A. Plymouth.

———◆———

Q. What was an opponent to the English Parliament called in Boston?

A. Boston Whig.

———◆———

Q. Whose last words were, "Thomas Jefferson still survives"?

A. John Adams.

———◆———

Q. What is the oldest building in Boston?

A. Paul Revere House (1676).

———◆———

Q. Who designed the Massachusetts State House in 1795?

A. Charles Bulfinch.

———◆———

Q. What Boston hall was destroyed by fire in 1762 and rebuilt using money from a lottery?

A. Faneuil Hall.

———◆———

Q. Where did President John F. Kennedy last use PT–796, the nation's last known operable World War II PT boat?

A. In his inaugural parade.

Q. What was the original name for Cambridge?

A. Newtowne.

Q. What woman was arrested in 1872 for trying to vote in the presidential election?

A. Susan B. Anthony.

Q. What United States city has a stadium named for Robert F. Kennedy?

A. Washington, D.C.

Q. What Bostonian was Richard Nixon's running mate in 1960?

A. Henry Cabot Lodge.

Q. What did the Sons of Liberty do on December 16, 1773?

A. Held the Boston Tea Party.

Q. What colony did Roger Williams leave in 1636 to escape oppression?

A. Massachusetts Bay.

Q. What Massachusetts native served as the United States Ambassador to the United Nations from 1953 until 1960?

A. Henry Cabot Lodge.

Q. What coinage series was minted by Massachusetts between 1653 and 1682?

A. Willow, Oak, and Pine tree coins.

Q. What three British ships were raided during the Boston Tea Party?

A. *Beaver, Dartmouth,* and *Eleanor.*

Q. What was the secret password to Boston's port during the war of 1812?

A. Grasshopper.

Q. What two Italian anarchists were executed for murder in Boston on August 23, 1927?

A. Nicollo Sacco and Bartolomeo Vanzetti.

Q. Who gave the opening address at Amherst College in 1821?

A. Noah Webster.

Q. In 1919, Gov. Coolidge broke a work strike by what Boston public servants?

A. Policemen.

Q. What was the nationality of the ship that collided with the *Andrea Doria* off the Massachusetts coast?

A. Swedish (the *Stockholm*).

Q. Of what type material is the Old Ship Church made?

A. Wood (in the design of a ship).

———◆———

Q. In what river did John Quincy Adams skinny-dip almost daily during his presidency?

A. Potomac.

———◆———

Q. What college did John Hancock attend?

A. Harvard.

———◆———

Q. What famous abolitionist and women's rights advocate was born on Nantucket Island in 1793?

A. Lucretia Coffin Mott.

———◆———

Q. What group does the Charlemont statue *Hail to the Sunrise* commemorate?

A. Mohawk Indians.

———◆———

Q. In what town is the homestead of Clara Barton, founder of the American Red Cross?

A. Oxford.

———◆———

Q. What great patriotic song did Falmouth-born Katherine Lee Bates write?

A. "America the Beautiful."

Q. What famous Bostonian was the first Postmaster General of the United States?

A. Benjamin Franklin.

———◆———

Q. The Cambridge home of what poet was used as Washington's headquarters during the Boston siege?

A. Henry Wadsworth Longfellow.

———◆———

Q. Who was elected to the House of Representatives after serving as United States president?

A. John Quincy Adams.

———◆———

Q. In 1843, what president attended the dedication of the Bunker Hill Monument in Massachusetts?

A. John Tyler.

———◆———

Q. What is the oldest commissioned warship afloat in the world?

A. USS *Constitution*.

———◆———

Q. For what was Grandma Moses known?

A. Her primitive painting style.

———◆———

Q. Lizzie Borden was convicted of what crime?

A. None (she was found innocent).

Q. What Boston building is often called the "Cradle of Liberty"?

A. Faneuil Hall.

———◆———

Q. What Massachusetts native was 71 years old when he signed the Declaration of Independence?

A. Benjamin Franklin.

———◆———

Q. In what Boston church was "America" first sung in 1832?

A. Park Street Church.

———◆———

Q. The cannons used to drive the British from Boston had been captured from what fort?

A. Ticonderoga.

———◆———

Q. What famous sculptor created the seated *Lincoln* in the Lincoln Memorial and the *Minuteman* in Concord?

A. Daniel Chester French.

———◆———

Q. At what famous fair were 383 sheep, 20 bulls, and 15 yoke of oxen sold for seventy dollars on October 1, 1810?

A. The First Agricultural Fair in Pittsfield.

———◆———

Q. What colonist was the commander at the Battle of Bunker Hill?

A. Colonel William Prescott.

Q. Two sons of what Boston family became president of the United States?

A. The Adams family.

———◆———

Q. In what famous meeting house were plans made for the Boston Tea Party?

A. Old South Meeting House.

———◆———

Q. What color was Lizzie Borden's hair?

A. Red.

———◆———

Q. Who was the first governor of Massachusetts under the Constitution completed in March 1780?

A. John Hancock.

———◆———

Q. Who was the sixth president of the United States?

A. John Quincy Adams.

———◆———

Q. Who was president of the United States when the United States Lighthouse Service was created?

A. George Washington.

———◆———

Q. From what chronic disorder did both Thomas Edison and Benjamin Franklin suffer?

A. Insomnia.

Q. What theft is known as the "robbery of the century"?

A. The Brinks Job.

———◆———

Q. What building was the first to display the United States flag in Colrain?

A. A public school.

———◆———

Q. What penalty was given to the men convicted of manslaughter during the Boston Massacre?

A. They were branded on the hand and set free.

———◆———

Q. How many of the British soldiers involved in the Boston Massacre were convicted of manslaughter?

A. Two.

———◆———

Q. Who was president of the Continental Congress in 1776?

A. John Hancock.

———◆———

Q. What United States president was elected by the House of Representatives because he did not win an electoral college majority?

A. John Quincy Adams.

———◆———

Q. In 1977, what two 1920s criminals did Gov. Michael Dukakis vindicate?

A. Nicollo Sacco and Bartolomeo Vanzetti.

Q. What kind of cannons did the *Mayflower* carry?

A. Sakerets.

---◆---

Q. In 1833, the first state hospital for the mentally ill opened in what city?

A. Worcester.

---◆---

Q. The first express service was organized in 1839 to run from Boston to what city?

A. New York.

---◆---

Q. What fruit did Ephraim Bull of Concord develop in 1849?

A. Concord grape.

---◆---

Q. In what kind of car was President Kennedy riding when he was assassinated?

A. 1961 Lincoln Continental.

---◆---

Q. For 35 years after the colonists arrived, what type of government existed in their New World?

A. Theocratic government.

---◆---

Q. What period of time did Lyndon Johnson declare as the official mourning period after the assassination of President Kennedy?

A. One month.

Q. What is painted on the only wooden World War II PT boat in the world that is on public display?

A. Shark's teeth (face).

---◆---

Q. According to legend, what pirate buried his treasure on Clarke's Island in Northfield?

A. Captain Kidd.

---◆---

Q. From what school at Boston University did Dr. Martin Luther King, Jr. receive his Ph.D?

A. The School of Theology

---◆---

Q. In what town is the Old Ship Church, the only seventeenth-century church left in Massachusetts, to be found?

A. Hingham.

---◆---

Q. The term *gerrymander* was developed, in part, from the name of what Massachusetts governor?

A. Eldridge Gerry.

---◆---

Q. In 1885, Captain Annie Shirley was the commander of the Maine and Massachusetts district of what army?

A. Salvation Army.

---◆---

Q. In 1620, the Wampanoag Indian campsite was situated near what colony?

A. Plymouth.

Q. Against what Republican did John F. Kennedy run in the 1960 election?

A. Richard Nixon.

Q. What national song was sung for the first time in Boston on July 4, 1832?

A. "America."

Q. Who was the colonists' leader when they held the Boston Tea Party?

A. Samuel Adams.

Q. How many people were sentenced to life in prison in connection with the Brinks robbery?

A. Eight.

Q. What was Paul Revere's profession?

A. Silversmith.

Q. What was provided for Boston Harbor by an act of the 1797 Congress?

A. 16 buoys.

Q. What agency was formed during the Kennedy administration to help developing nations?

A. The Peace Corps.

Q. On whose memorial is written, "I believe it is important for this country to sail and not lie still in the harbor"?

A. John F. Kennedy.

------◆------

Q. What justice of the United States Supreme Court, born in Boston in 1841, resigned when he was almost 91 years old?

A. Oliver Wendell Holmes, Jr.

------◆------

Q. Although he was a Democrat Republican in the 1824 election, what type of Republican was John Quincy Adams in the 1828 election?

A. A National Republican.

------◆------

Q. In 1919, what man was imprisoned after exploiting millions from Boston investors with a "get-rich-quick" scheme?

A. Charles Ponzi.

------◆------

Q. In what city did the gruesome murder of Lizzie Borden's parents take place?

A. Fall River.

------◆------

Q. What was Joseph P. Kennedy, Jr., doing when he died in 1944?

A. Flying a B–24 bomber.

------◆------

Q. What sewing machine manufacturer started his company in Boston in 1851?

A. L. M. Singer.

Q. Where is the oldest flag in the United States?

A. The Bedford Public Library.

———◆———

Q. How old was John F. Kennedy when he was inaugurated as president in 1961?

A. 43.

———◆———

Q. In March 1770, what objects thrown at customs house sentries resulted in the Boston Massacre?

A. Snowballs.

———◆———

Q. Who was George Washington's vice president?

A. John Adams.

———◆———

Q. What judge ordered the integration of Boston's schools in 1974?

A. Federal Judge W. Arthur Garrity.

———◆———

Q. How many months each year were Shaker children required to attend school?

A. Four.

———◆———

Q. What was the name of the horse Paul Revere borrowed when he carried the warning of the British invasion?

A. Brown Beauty.

Q. What was the maiden name of John Hancock's wife?

A. Dorothy Quincy.

Q. In colonial times, where did wealthy, socially prominent Boston families live?

A. Beacon Hill.

Q. Erected in 1824, what Plymouth museum is said to be the oldest in the country?

A. Pilgrim Hall.

Q. Who was the first United States president to be born in the twentieth century?

A. John F. Kennedy.

Q. How old was Paul Revere when he made his famous midnight ride?

A. 40.

Q. In what city was President Kennedy shot?

A. Dallas.

Q. Where was Roger Williams ordered to go after being banished from Massachusetts?

A. England.

Q. What church founded Harvard College to provide a well-educated clergy?

A. Puritan (later Congregational).

———◆———

Q. What form of the arts was banned in Boston from 1750 to 1794?

A. Stage drama.

———◆———

Q. What college was opened in 1837 by Mary Lyon as the first women's college in America?

A. Mount Holyoke.

———◆———

Q. To what city did the British sail after being evacuated from Boston in March 1776?

A. Halifax, Nova Scotia.

———◆———

Q. What famous captain was taken from Boston to England to be hanged as a pirate and murderer in 1701?

A. Captain William Kidd.

———◆———

Q. About how many slaves were in Massachusetts in 1680?

A. 100.

———◆———

Q. What cardinal of the Roman Catholic church officiated at the burial service for John F. Kennedy?

A. Richard Cardinal Cushing.

Q. The steeple of what famous Boston church fell during a hurricane in 1955?

A. Old North Church.

◆

Q. What is the oldest town on Martha's Vineyard?

A. Edgartown.

◆

Q. About what event did John Adams say, "On that night the foundation of American independence was laid"?

A. The Boston Massacre.

◆

Q. Who said, "One man can make a difference and every man should try"?

A. John F. Kennedy.

◆

Q. What Brookline resident ran for president of the United States in 1988?

A. Michael S. Dukakis.

◆

Q. On what bridge was fired the "shot heard around the world"?

A. North Bridge, Concord.

◆

Q. When the Pilgrims arrived in New England, what common eating utensil did they lack?

A. The fork.

Q. What literary magazine did a group of Transcendentalists publish in the mid–1800s in Concord?

A. *The Dial.*

———◆———

Q. Samuel Sewall was a stern trial judge during what notorious episode in American history?

A. Salem witch trials.

———◆———

Q. What religious group, which migrated from England to America in 1774, practiced celibacy, community property, and simplicity?

A. Shakers.

———◆———

Q. What is pottage, a common dish among the early settlers?

A. Soup.

———◆———

Q. The XYZ Affair, which occurred during John Adams' presidency, involved agents of what nationality?

A. French.

———◆———

Q. What town was originally planned to be the capital of Massachusetts Bay?

A. Cambridge.

———◆———

Q. Who was the defense lawyer for the British soldiers involved in the Boston Massacre?

A. John Adams.

Q. Who was the second United States president to be buried in Arlington National Cemetery?

A. John F. Kennedy.

———◆———

Q. What Italian ocean liner sank off the coast of Massachusetts in 1956?

A. *Andrea Doria.*

———◆———

Q. To whom did John Quincy Adams lose the 1828 presidential election?

A. Andrew Jackson.

———◆———

Q. What holiday is celebrated on June 18 in Suffolk County?

A. Bunker Hill Day.

———◆———

Q. Who was dubbed the "Napoleon of the women's rights movement"?

A. Susan B. Anthony.

———◆———

Q. On the *Mayflower*, what did the shipstaff move?
A. The tiller.

———◆———

Q. Mary Chilton was the first woman to step on what landmark?

A. Plymouth Rock.

Q. John Adams is credited with the founding of what branch of the military?

A. The United States Marine Corps (1798).

———◆———

Q. What was America's first written constitution, drawn up by the Pilgrims?

A. The Mayflower Compact.

———◆———

Q. What was the Boston subway first called?

A. Tremont Street Subway.

———◆———

Q. What is the first name of Gov. Michael Dukakis's wife?

A. Kitty.

———◆———

Q. What leader of the women's rights movement was born in Adams in 1820?

A. Susan B. Anthony.

———◆———

Q. At what age did Benjamin Franklin leave Boston and move to Philadelphia?

A. 17.

———◆———

Q. How many shots were fired at President John F. Kennedy?

A. Three.

Q. What two men completed Paul Revere's ride after he was captured?

A. Samuel Prescott and William Dawes.

———◆———

Q. What word did Susan B. Anthony want to eliminate from state constitutions?

A. *Male.*

———◆———

Q. What Massachusetts woman did Ronald Reagan appoint as Secretary of Health and Human Services in 1983?

A. Margaret M. Heckler.

———◆———

Q. What man was known as the "father of the American Revolution"?

A. Samuel Adams.

———◆———

Q. Who was the last signer of the Mayflower Compact to die?

A. John Alden.

———◆———

Q. What type of sailing vessel did John Alden design?

A. Sloop.

———◆———

Q. In what river was the entire navy of Massachusetts destroyed in 1779?

A. Penobscot (Maine).

Q. In an Indian village in Plymouth, what was a *wetu*?

A. A home.

---◆---

Q. What was the first book printed in the English colonies?

A. *The Bay Psalm Book.*

---◆---

Q. Gloucester was the first site to make what type of fore-and-aft rigged ship?

A. Schooner.

---◆---

Q. What assassin shot John F. Kennedy?

A. Lee Harvey Oswald.

---◆---

Q. On what hill was the Battle of Bunker Hill fought?

A. Breed's Hill.

---◆---

Q. Under the auspices of what church was Boston University founded in 1839?

A. Methodist.

---◆---

Q. Who drafted the original Massachusetts constitution?

A. John Adams.

Q. Whom did John F. Kennedy appoint as Attorney General in 1961?

A. Robert F. Kennedy.

Q. What Great Barrington native helped found the NAACP?

A. William E. B. DuBois.

Q. Robert F. Kennedy was United States senator from what state?

A. New York.

Q. In 1786, a group of farmers unable to pay their debts rose up in rebellion under whose leadership?

A. Captain Daniel Shays.

Q. What was hidden in Boston's Park Street Church for use during the War of 1812?

A. Gunpowder.

Q. On April 18, 1975, what United States president launched America's Bicentennial at Boston's Old North Church?

A. Gerald Ford.

Q. What Bostonian served as secretary of state under James Monroe?

A. John Quincy Adams.

Q. During the 1700s, Edwards Pond was used for the "drown if you're innocent, float if you're guilty" test for people accused of what crime?

A. Witchcraft.

Q. The destroyer *J. P. Kennedy, Jr.,* is the official Massachusetts state memorial to those who died in what two wars?

A. Korean and Vietnam.

Q. Who was John Adams' vice president?

A. Thomas Jefferson.

Q. What Boston merchant was the first person to sign the Declaration of Independence?

A. John Hancock.

Q. In 1961, President Kennedy appointed R. Sargent Shriver as director of what program?

A. The Peace Corps.

Q. Amos Kendall, born in Dunstable, was a member of what informal group of counselors to President Andrew Jackson?

A. The Kitchen Cabinet.

Q. Where did Jacqueline and John F. Kennedy have their wedding reception?

A. Hammersmith Farm.

Q. Who was made president of the first legally established Board of Health in America, February 13, 1799?

A. Paul Revere.

———————◆———————

Q. What two Boston uprisings were caused by taxation without representation?

A. The Boston Massacre and the Boston Tea Party.

———————◆———————

Q. What was the cost of the site of Andover?

A. Six pounds and an old coat.

———————◆———————

Q. Who supplied the brass fittings for the frigate known as "Old Ironsides"?

A. Paul Revere.

———————◆———————

Q. What products were manufactured by Oliver Ames and Sons in their Massachusetts factory?

A. Shovels.

———————◆———————

Q. Who won the Battle of Bunker Hill?

A. The British.

———————◆———————

Q. What king made Massachusetts a royal colony in 1684?

A. King James II.

Q. What president of the United States lived in Quincy?

A. John Quincy Adams.

———◆———

Q. Who destroyed the settlement in Deerfield in 1675, and again in 1704?

A. Indians.

———◆———

Q. What colonist was elected governor before he left England?

A. John Winthrop.

———◆———

Q. Who was the first Roman Catholic to be elected president of the United States?

A. John F. Kennedy.

———◆———

Q. Who used Poor Richard as a pen name?

A. Benjamin Franklin.

———◆———

Q. Who did John Adams suggest for commander-in-chief of the American army?

A. George Washington.

———◆———

Q. What early United States vice president called that position "the most insignificant office that ever the invention of man contrived or his imagination conceived"?

A. John Adams.

Q. What did President John Adams drink almost every morning of his adult life?

A. Hard cider.

◆

Q. In 1927, what did the United States submarine S–4 hit that made it sink off Provincetown?

A. A Coast Guard destroyer.

◆

Q. Whose signature is largest on the Declaration of Independence?

A. John Hancock's.

◆

Q. What is the present name of the area once known as *Shawmut* to the Indians of the Algonquin nation?

A. Boston.

◆

Q. In 1620, what did the Pilgrims call their new settlement?

A. Plimoth Plantation.

◆

Q. What man from Massachusetts did Richard Nixon appoint as Secretary of Defense in 1973?

A. Elliot Richardson.

◆

Q. The National Monument of the Forefathers, Plymouth, served as a prototype for what United States statue?

A. The Statue of Liberty.

Q. In 1796, John Adams was elected president as a member of what party?

A. Federalist.

———◆———

Q. At what college were the first twelve freshmen enrolled in the summer of 1638?

A. Harvard.

———◆———

Q. What town refers to itself as the "Birthplace of American Liberty"?

A. Lexington.

———◆———

Q. Why was Ethan Allen kicked out of Northampton in 1765?

A. For drinking too much.

———◆———

Q. At what tavern did the colonial patriots gather in 1773, just before the Boston Tea Party?

A. Green Dragon.

———◆———

Q. What religious sect called their settlement "The City of Peace"?

A. The Shakers.

———◆———

Q. What was the religious affiliation of John Adams and John Quincy Adams?

A. Unitarian.

Q. What Native Americans are living and preserving their history on the Hassanamisco Reservation in Grafton?

A. The Nipmuc.

———◆———

Q. Who shot Senator Robert F. Kennedy in 1968?

A. Sirhan Bishara Sirhan.

———◆———

Q. A circle of paving stones outside Boston's Old State House marks the spot of what 1770 event?

A. The Boston Massacre.

———◆———

Q. After Massachusetts native and women's rights pioneer Lucy Stone married Henry Blackwell in 1855, how was she addressed?

A. Mrs. Stone.

———◆———

Q. Where was the Declaration of Independence first read in Boston?

A. The Old State House.

———◆———

Q. In what month did Paul Revere's midnight ride occur?

A. April.

———◆———

Q. What part of John Quincy Adams' body was malformed, due to a childhood accident?

A. His right arm.

Q. In 1842, a Massachusetts law was passed limiting children under twelve to how many working hours per day?

A. Ten.

———◆———

Q. What did Paul Revere wear every day after the Revolutionary War until his death?

A. His uniform.

———◆———

Q. What colonel arrived in Cambridge in 1776 with 43 cannons and 16 mortars?

A. Colonel Henry Knox.

———◆———

Q. In 1900, what percentage of the boots and shoes manufactured in the country came from Massachusetts?

A. 50 percent.

———◆———

Q. What state passed the first minimum-wage law?

A. Massachusetts.

———◆———

Q. For what was the Sabbath Circle used as a symbol?

A. Witchcraft.

———◆———

Q. What did colonial New Englanders mean when they said a person "clawed-off" or "clawed-out"?

A. The person made excuses.

Q. In what city was the nation's first jewelry manufacturing business, founded in 1780?

A. Attleboro.

———◆———

Q. The Shakers' "fingered" lap boxes were made in how many sizes?

A. 15.

———◆———

Q. What was the name of General Douglas MacArthur's father, born in Chicopee?

A. Arthur MacArthur.

———◆———

Q. How many Boston citizens were killed at the Boston Massacre?

A. Five.

———◆———

Q. How many times was John Winthrop, the first Massachusetts Bay governor, married?

A. Four.

———◆———

Q. How were wagons pulled on the first railroad in America, built in Quincy?

A. By horse.

———◆———

Q. What New Englander thought we should drop the letters C, J, Q, W, and Y from the alphabet and substitute other symbols for them?

A. Benjamin Franklin.

Q. In 1864, what weapon did the Springfield Armory produce 1,000 of every day?

A. Muskets.

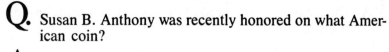

Q. Susan B. Anthony was recently honored on what American coin?

A. The one-dollar piece.

Q. What coin did the Massachusetts colony first issue?

A. Three-pence.

Q. Who covered the wood dome of Boston's State House with copper?

A. Paul Revere.

Q. What "first-in-America" transportation system opened in Boston in 1898?

A. The subway.

Q. What was Air Force One's nickname when John F. Kennedy was president?

A. "Caroline."

Q. How did King C. Gillette of Massachusetts make a living before he invented the disposable razor?

A. He was a bottle cap salesman.

Q. How long did the Pilgrim voyage to New England take?

A. 66 days.

———◆———

Q. How many women did the Boston Strangler kill?

A. 13.

———◆———

Q. Where did the Pilgrims originally plan to settle in the New World?

A. Virginia.

———◆———

Q. Pilgrims were called "Puritan Separatists" because they wanted to cut ties with what organization?

A. The Church of England.

———◆———

Q. What was in the center of the flag used by the sons of Liberty?

A. A green pine tree.

———◆———

Q. What Indians were almost annihilated during a battle against Plymouth and Connecticut colonies in 1675?

A. Narragansett.

———◆———

Q. To the eastern Indians, what berries were known as *sassamanesh*?

A. Cranberries.

Q. What is sallets, which the Pilgrims served at the first Thanksgiving feast?

A. A vegetable dish.

———◆———

Q. What kind of fishing ships were the *Acushnet* and the *Pequod*?

A. Whaling ships.

———◆———

Q. For what did the Pilgrims make an appropriation out of their funds, ten years after they landed?

A. A college.

———◆———

Q. How many Pilgrims returned to England after their first winter, when about half of them died?

A. None.

———◆———

Q. What day is observed as Forefather's Day in New England?

A. December 21.

———◆———

Q. How many days did the first Thanksgiving feast and celebration last?

A. Three.

———◆———

Q. What did the colonists call a "lucifer"?

A. A kitchen match.

ARTS & LITERATURE

C H A P T E R   F O U R

Q. For what book did John F. Kennedy win the Pulitzer Prize for non-fiction?

A. *Profiles in Courage.*

------◆------

Q. For what audience did Anne Sexton and Maxine Kumin write books together?

A. Children and young adults.

------◆------

Q. On the search for Moby Dick, Queequeg carried with him the wooden statue of what god?

A. Yojo.

------◆------

Q. What was the pond on which Henry David Thoreau lived in a small cabin?

A. Walden Pond.

------◆------

Q. At what college is the Sterling and Francis Clark Art Museum to be found?

A. Williams.

Q. Who wrote, "Nothing is certain but death and taxes"?

A. Benjamin Franklin.

———————◆———————

Q. What 1867 Boston newspaper was the first to be printed on wood-pulp paper?

A. *The Morning Journal.*

———————◆———————

Q. What Massachusetts author was noted for her works about nature, animals, and their relationship to humans?

A. Maxine Kumin.

———————◆———————

Q. What play was based on the Sacco-Vanzetti case?

A. *Winterset.*

———————◆———————

Q. Where was Edgar Allan Poe born?

A. Boston.

———————◆———————

Q. What Cambridge-born speaker of the United States House of Representatives was known as "Tip"?

A. Thomas P. O'Neill.

———————◆———————

Q. What Congregational minister, born in 1663, wrote a book in which he sanctioned the persecution of witches in Salem?

A. Cotton Mather.

Q. Sylvia Plath's *The Bell Jar* was originally published under what pseudonym?

A. Victoria Lucas.

———◆———

Q. Where did author Herman Melville settle?

A. Pittsfield.

———◆———

Q. The Isabella Stewart Gardner Museum in Boston was built in what architectural style?

A. Italian.

———◆———

Q. What conductor of the Boston Symphony Orchestra referred to Beethoven's Fifth Symphony as a "fifth of Beethoven"?

A. Arthur Fiedler.

———◆———

Q. In 1954, what two words did Congress add to the original Pledge of Allegiance, which had been printed by Boston's *Youth Companion* magazine?

A. *Under God.*

———◆———

Q. What famous writer wrote, "Who hears the fishes when they cry?"

A. Thoreau.

———◆———

Q. In 1875, what women's college opened its doors 24 hours ahead of Smith College?

A. Wellesley College.

Q. What work won Massachusetts-born Elizabeth Bishop the Pulitzer Prize?

A. *North and South—A Cold Spring.*

✦

Q. What internationally known newspaper was founded by Mary Baker Eddy?

A. *The Christian Science Monitor.*

✦

Q. Who wrote *Walden?*

A. Henry David Thoreau.

✦

Q. What party did Kevin White represent while he was mayor of Boston?

A. The Democratic Party.

✦

Q. What is the highest academic degree awarded by the College of the Holy Cross in Worcester?

A. Bachelor.

✦

Q. What famous writer used the pen names A. M. Barnard and Flora Fairfield?

A. Louisa May Alcott.

✦

Q. What city did Gilbert Stuart call the "Athens of America"?

A. Philadelphia.

Q. Gloucester is the setting for what Rudyard Kipling novel?

A. *Captains Courageous.*

--------◆--------

Q. What five colleges are in the western Massachusetts exchange program?

A. University of Massachusetts, Amherst, Mount Holyoke, Hampshire, and Smith.

--------◆--------

Q. What Boston artist painted portraits of the king and queen of England as well as *Death of Chatham?*

A. John Singleton Copley.

--------◆--------

Q. Where is Hopkins Observatory, the oldest college observatory in the United States?

A. Williams College, Williamstown.

--------◆--------

Q. What college was founded by Sophia Smith?

A. Smith.

--------◆--------

Q. Who wrote *Love Story,* in which much of the action takes place in Cambridge?

A. Erich Segal.

--------◆--------

Q. How many of Emily Dickinson's poems were published during her lifetime?

A. Five.

Q. Who was the captain of the *Pequod* in Melville's *Moby Dick?*

A. Ahab.

---◆---

Q. What famous poet was referred to as the "nun of Amherst"?

A. Emily Dickinson.

---◆---

Q. What New England newspaper won the Pulitzer Prize for photography in 1976, 1977, and 1979?

A. *The Boston Herald-American.*

---◆---

Q. Who wrote and sang "Alice's Restaurant," which was set in Stockbridge?

A. Arlo Guthrie.

---◆---

Q. From what Massachusetts school did Helen Keller and her teacher, Anne Mansfield Sullivan, graduate?

A. The Perkins School for the Blind.

---◆---

Q. What Haverhill poet wrote *Snow Bound*?

A. John Greenleaf Whittier.

---◆---

Q. What Springfield native wrote *The Butter Battle Book*, which was on the best-seller list for a year?

A. Dr. Seuss (Theodore Giesel).

Q. What college did John Simmons found in 1899?

A. Simmons.

◆

Q. From what island did Edgar Allan Poe get his idea for the setting of "The Cask of Amontillado"?

A. Castle Island.

◆

Q. What Lowell-born artist painted *Portrait of My Mother*?

A. James Whistler.

◆

Q. Where was Gilbert Stuart buried?

A. In the Boston Common.

◆

Q. What was Hester Prynne sentenced to wear in Nathaniel Hawthorne's *The Scarlet Letter*?

A. The letter A.

◆

Q. What Sylvia Plath poem portrayed her mother?

A. "The Disquieting Muses."

◆

Q. Longfellow wrote *The Wreck of the Hesperus* after being inspired by the shipwrecks on what reef?

A. Norman's Woe, Gloucester.

Q. What college was the first university in America?

A. Harvard.

———◆———

Q. What Boston-born author is regarded by some as the father of the short story, the detective story, and the horror story?

A. Edgar Allan Poe.

———◆———

Q. On April 3, 1776, what did George Washington receive from Harvard?

A. An honorary degree.

———◆———

Q. Who created a Boston palace (now a museum) on the Fenway?

A. Isabella Stewart Gardner.

———◆———

Q. What was the name of Herman Melville's home near Pittsfield?

A. Arrowhead.

———◆———

Q. What three major downtown Boston theaters are famous for pre-Broadway premieres?

A. Wilbur, Shubert, and Colonial.

———◆———

Q. What profession in Amherst employs the most people?

A. Education.

Q. Who wrote "Ballad of a Strange Thing"?

A. H. Phelps Putnam.

———◆———

Q. Of what Irish city was Gilbert Stuart fond?

A. Dublin.

———◆———

Q. Who was the first Harvard professor of modern languages?

A. George Ticknor.

———◆———

Q. What Massachusetts school is the largest independent boarding school in the continental United States?

A. Northfield-Mount Herman School.

———◆———

Q. What United States secretary of education was one of Williams College's most noted alumni?

A. William Bennett.

———◆———

Q. How did Gilbert Stuart's father earn a living?

A. He was a snuff-grinder.

———◆———

Q. What magazine published Sylvia Plath's first short story, "And Summer Will Not Come Again"?

A. *Seventeen.*

Q. What distinction does Massachusetts poet Phillis Wheatley hold?

A. America's first published black woman poet.

Q. What Henry David Thoreau book was based on his walking trips on Cape Cod?

A. *Cape Cod.*

Q. What prep school did John F. Kennedy and Adlai Stevenson attend?

A. Choate-Rosemary Hall.

Q. What university was the first in the world to open all departments to women?

A. Boston University.

Q. What college did Robert Frost attend during the 1920s?

A. Amherst.

Q. The Harvard Annex, which provided education for women, is now known by what name?

A. Radcliffe.

Q. Where was artist Winslow Homer born?

A. Boston.

Q. What request of the Academy of Florence did Gilbert Stuart refuse to grant?

A. To paint a self-portrait.

———◆———

Q. What college did Nathaniel Hawthorne attend?

A. Bowdoin.

———◆———

Q. What supplement to the *Boston Herald* was abandoned in 1908, but later reinstated?

A. The comics.

———◆———

Q. What story did Nathaniel Hawthorne burn because he could not find a publisher?

A. "Seven Tales of My Native Land."

———◆———

Q. What drug was first developed as a surgical anesthetic by Dr. William Morton of Charlton?

A. Ether.

———◆———

Q. The poem "Manners (for a Child of 1918)" describes the feelings Elizabeth Bishop had for what relative?

A. Her grandfather.

———◆———

Q. What is the highest academic degree conferred by Boston University?

A. Doctorate.

Q. Who created the fictional detective C. Auguste Dupin?

A. Edgar Allan Poe.

———◆———

Q. What famous painting by A. M. Willard is now in Abbot Hall?

A. *The Spirit of '76.*

———◆———

Q. Oliver Wendell Holmes, Henry Wadsworth Longfellow, and James Russell Lowell were known as the "Boston Brahmins," a phrase coined by whom?

A. Holmes.

———◆———

Q. What magazine paid Sylvia Plath's first professional earnings of $100.00?

A. *Harper's.*

———◆———

Q. What "patriarch of Quincy" claimed he would be glad to sit for Gilbert Stuart from one year's end to another?

A. John Adams.

———◆———

Q. What was invented by John Robert Gregg, an Irishman who moved to Boston in 1893?

A. The Gregg System of Shorthand.

———◆———

Q. What is the largest privately endowed liberal arts college for women in the United States?

A. Smith.

Q. Astronomer William Cranch Bond, who discovered the Great Comet of 1811, was the first director of what college observatory?

A. Harvard.

Q. Who became Boston's Roman Catholic cardinal in 1985?

A. Cardinal Law.

Q. Who wrote, "For a few outward successes I may seem to have, there are acres of misgivings and self-doubt"?

A. Sylvia Plath.

Q. In what town did Nathaniel Hawthorne grow up?

A. Salem.

Q. How much money did Isabella Stewart Gardner receive for the Walt Whitman Citation of Merit award?

A. $10,000.

Q. To whom did Isabella Gardner give her $10,000 award?

A. Yaddo (a creative artists colony in New York).

Q. What Harvard graduate wrote "The Dry Salvages"?

A. T. S. Eliot.

Q. What would Gilbert Stuart do if his subject fell asleep during a sitting?

A. Paint ass's ears on the portrait.

Q. Where did Sylvia Plath get the title "Ocean 1212-W" for one of her poems?

A. Her telephone number.

Q. What university in Waltham was named after a justice of the United States Supreme Court?

A. Brandeis.

Q. From what educational institution did Rose Kennedy and Coretta Scott King graduate?

A. New England Conservatory.

Q. What famous poet lived in "the Mansion," in Amherst?

A. Emily Dickinson.

Q. What book did Louisa May Alcott originally title *The Pathetic Family*?

A. *Little Women.*

Q. What Robert McCloskey book is about duck parents that made their home in the Boston Public Garden?

A. *Make Way for Ducklings.*

Q. What New England university library has more than ten million bound volumes?

A. Harvard.

---◆---

Q. In what town did Alcott, Hawthorne, Thoreau, and Emerson all reside at some time?

A. Concord.

---◆---

Q. What Elizabeth Bishop short story was published in the *Partisan Review* only four years after her high school graduation?

A. "In Prison."

---◆---

Q. How many times did Isabella Stewart Gardner marry?

A. Four.

---◆---

Q. How long did Nathaniel Hawthorne live in a "haunted" room and refuse to go outside during the day?

A. Eleven years.

---◆---

Q. What is the art of engraving whale's teeth called?

A. Scrimshaw.

---◆---

Q. What was Anne Sexton's first book?

A. *To Bedlam and Part Way Back.*

Q. To what British tune is the song "America" sung?

A. "God Save the King/Queen."

———◆———

Q. What are the four New England Ivy League colleges?

A. Harvard, Brown, Dartmouth, and Yale.

———◆———

Q. What is the oldest free municipal library in the world?

A. Boston Public Library.

———◆———

Q. What New England newspaper has the largest circulation?

A. *Boston Globe.*

———◆———

Q. How many faculty members does Harvard employ for its 17,000 students?

A. 1,693.

———◆———

Q. What is the largest high school in the northeast?

A. Brockton High School.

———◆———

Q. What military academy expelled native Bostonian Edgar Allan Poe?

A. West Point.

Q. What did Ralph Nader do in the United States Army?

A. Cook.

◆

Q. What is pictured on the back of the currency note that shows Benjamin Franklin's portrait?

A. Independence Hall.

◆

Q. What is the Mary Garden, found in Woods Hole?

A. A garden of plants with names associated with the Virgin Mary.

◆

Q. In what city was the first road map for public use published in 1698?

A. Boston.

◆

Q. What illness afflicted Elizabeth Bishop her entire life?

A. Asthma.

◆

Q. Who said, "A work of genius. It signifies a moment of major importance to American literature," in reference to Anne Sexton's first book?

A. James Wright.

◆

Q. On what condition did Sarah Whitman agree to marry Edgar Allan Poe?

A. That he stop drinking.

Q. Why did Gilbert Stuart refuse to allow a Boston exhibit of his pictures to open?

A. Because they were badly hung.

———◆———

Q. In what year did the first volume of Emily Dickinson's poems appear?

A. 1890.

———◆———

Q. What was Nathaniel Hawthorne's nickname at college?

A. Oberon.

———◆———

Q. What was Anne Sexton's profession before she began writing?

A. Fashion model.

———◆———

Q. What town was Isabella Stewart Gardner referring to in her poem, "Summer Remembered"?

A. Easthampton.

———◆———

Q. What did Henry David Thoreau's father do for a living?

A. He was a pencil-maker.

———◆———

Q. Paul Szep, who worked for the *Boston Globe*, won Pulitzer prizes in 1974 and 1977 for what work?

A. His cartoons.

Q. Who was a former pastor of a Boston church and son of the Reverend William Emerson?

A. Ralph Waldo Emerson.

◆

Q. Where did Longfellow live in Cambridge?

A. At the Craigie House.

◆

Q. Where is the American Antiquarian Society?

A. Worcester.

◆

Q. Who is best known for the many fine pastels of Massachusetts people he drew during the Revolutionary period?

A. Benjamin Blyth.

◆

Q. What itinerant painter of the early 1800s also practiced for 27 years as the only physician in Duxbury?

A. Rufus Hathaway.

◆

Q. What painter became an instructor of the deaf and mute artist John Brewster, Jr.?

A. Joseph Steward.

◆

Q. What was the first public school in the country?

A. Boston Public Latin School.

Q. Elizabeth Bishop's grandfather was responsible for the construction of what two famous Boston buildings?

A. The Boston Public Library and the Museum of Fine Arts.

———◆———

Q. What type of paintings were done by John Johnston?

A. Portraits.

———◆———

Q. Who wrote *Outre-Mer*?

A. Longfellow.

———◆———

Q. In what Elizabeth Bishop poem did she portray her Uncle George, who ran away to sea at the age of 14 and later became a painter?

A. "Large Bad Picture."

———◆———

Q. What New England architect designed the U.S. Capitol in Washington, DC?

A. Charles Bulfinch.

———◆———

Q. In what hospital was Sylvia Plath born?

A. Boston Memorial.

———◆———

Q. Who wrote "Are Poets Ballplayers?"

A. Isabella Stewart Gardner.

Q. How did Sylvia Plath die?

A. Suicide.

———◆———

Q. What was H. Phelps Putnam's first book?

A. *Trinc*.

———◆———

Q. What poet wrote "Sylvia's Death" six days after Sylvia Plath died?

A. Anne Sexton.

———◆———

Q. What does Anne Sexton reveal about her father in "All My Pretty Ones"?

A. He was an alcoholic.

———◆———

Q. To whom was Richard Moore referring when he called her "an accomplished and professional poet of what might be called the Bishop-Lowell-Sexton school"?

A. Maxine Kumin.

———◆———

Q. What award did Anne Sexton receive in 1967?

A. Pulitzer Prize for poetry.

———◆———

Q. In 1972, Maxine Kumin won the Pulitzer Prize for what book?

A. *Up Country: Poems of New England*.

Q. What famous hymn did Boston's Julia Ward Howe write?

A. "Battle Hymn of the Republic."

———◆———

Q. How many museums make up the quadrangle in Springfield?

A. Four.

———◆———

Q. Who was the model for John Singer Sargent's painting, *Madame X*?

A. Isabella Stewart Gardner.

———◆———

Q. What did Isabella Stewart Gardner want to be before she began writing poetry?

A. An actress.

———◆———

Q. What symphony calls the Great Woods Center for the Performing Arts its summer home?

A. Pittsburgh Symphony.

———◆———

Q. How many poems were found after Emily Dickinson's death?

A. More than 1,200.

———◆———

Q. Who wrote "Murders in the Rue Morgue," one of the first-known published short stories?

A. Edgar Allan Poe.

Q. In what publication was Amy Lowell's first verse printed?

A. *The Atlantic Monthly.*

Q. What is the name of Edward Cummings' first book?

A. *Tulips and Chimneys.*

Q. Where did writer H. Phelps Putnam attend college?

A. Yale.

Q. Who wrote, "One man lies in his words and gets a bad reputation; another in his manners, and enjoys a good one"?

A. Thoreau.

Q. *Birthdays from the Ocean* is the title of what poet's first book?

A. Isabella Stewart Gardner.

Q. Who wrote *The Rise of the Dutch Republic,* published in 1856?

A. John Lathrop Motley.

Q. Where did John Harvard receive his "signatures"?

A. Emmanuel College, England.

Q. What museum has 58 works by John Singleton Copley?

A. The Museum of Fine Arts.

———◆———

Q. In what way did Boston pay tribute to the children's classic, *Make Way for Ducklings?*

A. Bronze statues of ducks in the park.

———◆———

Q. What did James McNeill Whistler's mother want him to be?

A. A minister.

SPORTS & LEISURE

CHAPTER FIVE

Q. With 3,667 points, what Boston Celtic player was once the all-time collegiate leading scorer?

A. Pete Maravich.

Q. What time do Red Sox night games usually begin?

A. 7:35 P.M.

Q. How many players were on each team during the first game of basketball in Springfield (December 1891)?

A. Nine.

Q. What sport did Derek Sanderson participate in after hockey?

A. Golf.

Q. What retired Boston Celtic player coached for two years at Regis College in Weston?

A. Dave Cowens.

Q. What university in Boston now uses the Red Sox's first grandstands, Huntington Avenue Grounds?

A. Northeastern.

Q. What is the most difficult hill encountered by participants in the Boston Marathon?

A. Heartbreak Hill.

Q. With a wild pitch in the tenth inning, what Red Sox pitcher helped lose the sixth game of the 1986 World Series?

A. Bob Stanley.

Q. What country club hosted the 1913 U.S. Open?

A. Brookline Country Club.

Q. What sport is played during the Beanpot Tournament?

A. Hockey.

Q. What position did Eddie Shore play for the Boston Bruins?

A. Defenseman.

Q. Who did the Boston Celtics beat in the 1984 NBA Championships?

A. The Los Angeles Lakers.

Q. What Red Sox player was the last major leaguer to hit over .400?

A. Ted Williams.

———◆———

Q. For what sports team did Jo Jo White play?

A. Boston Celtics.

———◆———

Q. What is the name of Boston College's football stadium?

A. Alumni Stadium.

———◆———

Q. What Cape Cod town hosts a televised road race of 7.1 miles?

A. Falmouth.

———◆———

Q. What Bruins goalie drew a stitch on his mask whenever a puck hit him?

A. Gerry Cheevers.

———◆———

Q. Since Harvard's first game, what is the regulation length of a football field?

A. 100 yards.

———◆———

Q. During the 1904 season, how many shutouts did Cy Young pitch?

A. Ten.

Q. What ski area is found in Montachusett?

A. Wachusett Mountain.

———◆———

Q. Where is the United States Figure Skating Museum and Hall of Fame?

A. Boston.

———◆———

Q. Who booted Wilson's grounder during the sixth game of the 1986 World Series?

A. Bill Buckner.

———◆———

Q. How many leaves are there on a Celtic clover?

A. Three.

———◆———

Q. In what town is Sullivan Stadium?

A. Foxboro.

———◆———

Q. Who sponsors the Boston Marathon?

A. Boston Athletic Association.

———◆———

Q. What New England Patriots player was voted 1971 Rookie of the Year?

A. Jim Plunkett.

Q. As of 1989, how many times had the Celtics been NBA champions?

A. Sixteen.

———◆———

Q. On the Quabbin Reservoir, what is the maximum number of people allowed in a boat?

A. Three.

———◆———

Q. In 1975, who won the Most Valuable Player award on the Red Sox team?

A. Fred Lynn.

———◆———

Q. What famous Red Sox player pitched three no-hitters in his lifetime?

A. Cy Young.

———◆———

Q. What two Celtics coaches had the nickname "Red"?

A. Red Auerbach and Dave Cowens.

———◆———

Q. In what year was the last All-Star baseball game held in Boston?

A. 1961.

———◆———

Q. What song did Jess Cain sing to commemorate the great season the Red Sox had in 1967?

A. "The Impossible Dream."

Q. For what event did James B. Connolly of Harvard win a gold medal in the 1896 Olympics?

A. The triple jump.

———◆———

Q. What color uniforms are used by the ushers at Fenway Park?

A. Red.

———◆———

Q. What 1981 Celtic playoff Most Valuable Player also has one of the highest lifetime field goal percentages?

A. Cedric Maxwell.

———◆———

Q. What Red Sox player won the Most Valuable Player award twice, the only Boston player to do this?

A. Ted Williams.

———◆———

Q. In 1968, Andre Vigar of Canada broke the World and Boston Marathon records in what class?

A. Wheelchair.

———◆———

Q. What Celtics player also signed contracts with the Dallas Cowboys and the Cincinnati Reds?

A. Jo Jo White.

———◆———

Q. In 1945, what New York football team merged with the Boston Yanks?

A. Brooklyn Tigers.

Q. What international sport did Harvard graduate Dwight Davis play?

A. Tennis.

Q. Karen Strives of Wellesley was a winner of the team gold medal at the 1984 Olympics with what partner?

A. Her horse, Ben Arthur.

Q. What is Red Auerbach's real first name?

A. Arnold.

Q. How many strikeouts did Cy Young have during his career?

A. 2,804.

Q. On December 12, 1899, what small piece of golf equipment was patented in Boston?

A. Golf tee.

Q. What Celtic was called "Elastic Man"?

A. Cedric Maxwell.

Q. What major league team has a Double A baseball team in Pittsfield?

A. The Cubs.

Q. What position did Bob Cousy play for the Celtics?

A. Guard.

Q. Where was the first Davis Cup tennis match played?

A. Longview Cricket Club, Boston.

Q. What did Carl Yastrzemski receive for his great performance in baseball in 1967?

A. The Triple Crown.

Q. In 1985, what role did Bob Cousy play at Celtics games?

A. Commentator.

Q. What sports series was sponsored by the Gillette Safety Razor Company when it was televised for the first time?

A. The World Series.

Q. Where did the game of baseball begin?

A. In the Springfield area.

Q. What four Celtic players have been chosen Playoff Most Valuable Players?

A. Larry Bird, Cedric Maxwell, Jo Jo White, and John Havlicek.

Q. What is the "green monster"?

A. The left field wall at Fenway Park.

———◆———

Q. What is the name of the Boston soccer team?

A. Boston Minutemen.

———◆———

Q. From what college did the Basketball Hall of Fame move to its present site along the Connecticut River?

A. Springfield.

———◆———

Q. What sport, invented in 1895 by Dr. Sargent of Harvard, is a combination of bowling, baseball, cricket, football, handball, and tennis?

A. Battle ball.

———◆———

Q. What team did the Boston Bruins lose to during the 1933 Stanley Cup playoffs after one hour, 44 minutes of overtime?

A. Toronto Maple Leafs.

———◆———

Q. What kind of ball was used in the first games of basketball played in Springfield?

A. Soccer ball.

———◆———

Q. What instrument did Celtics player Tony Laveli often play at half time?

A. Accordion.

Q. What was the name of Boston's team when it played its first major league baseball game?

A. Boston Red Stockings.

Q. What was John Havlicek's nickname?

A. "Hondo."

Q. How many times was Ted Williams the American League home run leader?

A. Four.

Q. In 1983, what woman set a world's record at the Boston marathon?

A. Joan Benoit.

Q. What sport is played at the Cadillac East Coast Open held in Hamilton?

A. Polo.

Q. What college won the NCAA Hockey Championship in 1949?

A. Boston College.

Q. What college hockey team tied with Minnesota for the most NCAA titles (3 each) during the 1970s?

A. Boston University.

Q. What ski area is in Milton?

A. Blue Hills.

———◆———

Q. In 1984, what Red Sox player hit the most home runs in the American League?

A. Tony Armas.

———◆———

Q. What two Celtic players were on the "All-League Team" and the "All-Defensive Team" in 1986?

A. Larry Bird and Kevin McHale.

———◆———

Q. What kind of meal is served to runners the night before the Boston Marathon?

A. Pasta.

———◆———

Q. From what New England college did Celtic Tom Heinsohn graduate in 1956?

A. College of the Holy Cross, Worcester.

———◆———

Q. What Red Sox player played more games for more years than any other player?

A. Carl Yastrzemski.

———◆———

Q. Phil Esposito was the first hockey player to use what type of hockey stick?

A. Curved.

Q. In the 1984–85 Celtic season what two players topped John Havlicek's one-game high score of 54 points?

A. Larry Bird and Kevin McHale.

———◆———

Q. How many off-road vehicle permits are issued each year by the Cape Cod National Seashore?

A. 3,000.

———◆———

Q. In 1961, what team won the All-Star baseball game held in Boston?

A. Neither (game called on account of rain).

———◆———

Q. To what team did the Boston Redskins lose the title in 1936?

A. Green Bay Packers.

———◆———

Q. What happened during Ted Williams' last time at bat in Fenway Park?

A. He hit a home run.

———◆———

Q. In 1980, what Celtics player was named NBA Rookie of the Year?

A. Larry Bird.

———◆———

Q. During Phil Esposito's 1,282 games, how many points did he score?

A. 1,590.

Q. With 28,000 square feet, where is the largest golf green in the world?

A. The International Golf Club, Bolton.

◆

Q. What are the Boston College football team colors?

A. Maroon and gold.

◆

Q. What New England professional sports team was dubbed the "Miracle Team" in 1914?

A. Boston Braves.

◆

Q. What Red Sox centerfielder was named to the All-Lefty Pro Baseball Team?

A. Fred Lynn.

◆

Q. What professional team used to be known as the Pilgrims?

A. Red Sox.

◆

Q. What was the USFL football team representing Boston?

A. Boston Breakers.

◆

Q. The Peach Basket Festival held in Springfield celebrates what sport?

A. Basketball.

Q. What Boston Bruins player won the Lady Byng Sportsmanship Trophy twice in the 1970s?

A. John Bucyk.

———◆———

Q. What great Celtic player participated in 1,270 games from 1963 to 1978?

A. John Havlicek.

———◆———

Q. During the first modern Olympic Games in 1896, an American from what college won the first gold medal?

A. Harvard.

———◆———

Q. Cy Young's nickname is a shortened form of what word?

A. Cyclone.

———◆———

Q. What did Oliver Wendell Holmes do for exercise every morning in Cambridge?

A. He rowed on the Charles River.

———◆———

Q. In 1972, what Red Sox catcher won the Rookie of the Year award?

A. Carlton Fisk.

———◆———

Q. Holyoke is the birthplace of what sport?

A. Volleyball.

Q. In 1970, what magazine voted Bobby Orr of the Bruins Sportsman of the Year?

A. *Sports Illustrated.*

———◆———

Q. What Boston player was the first to hit four home runs in one game?

A. Robert L. Lowe.

———◆———

Q. In 1918, the Boston Marathon was cancelled for what reason?

A. World War I.

———◆———

Q. The Eagles is the name of what New England college football team?

A. Boston College.

———◆———

Q. Who was honored as the Bruins' leading goalie in 1983?

A. Pete Peters.

———◆———

Q. What was the final score of the Chicago/New England 1985 Super Bowl, the second most decisive win in Super Bowl history?

A. Chicago 46–New England 10.

———◆———

Q. What caused the Boston Bulldogs football team to disband in 1930?

A. The Depression.

Q. Dr. James Naismith organized and started what major sport?

A. Basketball.

———◆———

Q. What Red Sox player won the Cy Young Award in 1967, the first year it was given specifically to an American League player?

A. Jim Lonborg.

———◆———

Q. What New England Patriots player rushed for 1,015 yards in the 1977 season?

A. Sam Cunningham.

———◆———

Q. What Red Sox pitcher was 24–4 during the 1986 season?

A. Roger Clemens.

———◆———

Q. Where does the Boston Marathon begin?

A. Hopkinton.

———◆———

Q. In what ranking did the Celtics end their first season?

A. Last.

———◆———

Q. What position did Bobby Orr usually play?

A. Defenseman.

Q. What men's professional golf tournament is held in Sutton?

A. Bank of Boston Classic.

———◆———

Q. Ken Harrelson of the Red Sox was the first player to wear what piece of equipment when at bat?

A. Golf glove.

———◆———

Q. What target sport originated in 1910 at Andover by a group of trapshooters?

A. Skeet shooting.

———◆———

Q. In the record-long 1920 baseball game between the Boston Braves and the Brooklyn Dodgers, how many innings were played?

A. 26.

———◆———

Q. How many yards did the Patriots rush for in the 1985 Super Bowl?

A. Seven.

———◆———

Q. Bruins Ray Bourque won what coveted trophy in 1980?

A. Calder Trophy for Best Rookie.

———◆———

Q. When a Red Sox game is canceled, a red light on what building flashes?

A. John Hancock Tower.

Q. What famous baseball player and manager was born Cornelius McGillicuddy in East Brookfield?

A. Connie Mack.

———◆———

Q. What was K. C. Jones' number, since retired?

A. 25.

———◆———

Q. What Celtic player was known as "Rapid Robert"?

A. Bob Cousy.

———◆———

Q. On what holiday does the Boston Marathon take place?

A. Patriots Day.

———◆———

Q. What three Boston colleges have served as home field for the New England Patriots?

A. Boston College, Boston University, and Harvard University.

———◆———

Q. What position did Jim Plunkett play on the New England Patriots team from 1971 to 1975?

A. Quarterback.

———◆———

Q. What town is ten miles from the starting point of the Boston Marathon?

A. Natick.

Q. The Wheat Thin Mayor's Cup is awarded during what kind of competition in Salem?

A. Bicycle racing.

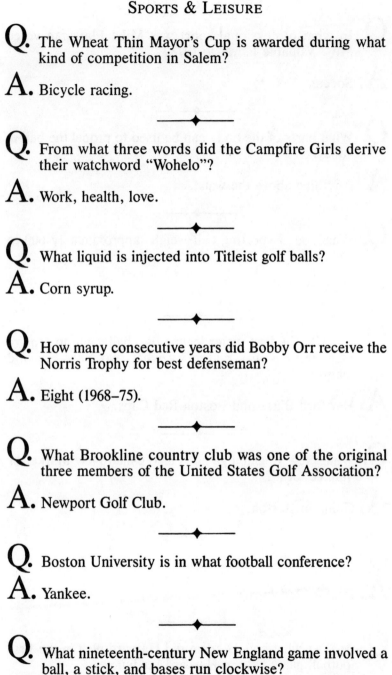

Q. From what three words did the Campfire Girls derive their watchword "Wohelo"?

A. Work, health, love.

Q. What liquid is injected into Titleist golf balls?

A. Corn syrup.

Q. How many consecutive years did Bobby Orr receive the Norris Trophy for best defenseman?

A. Eight (1968–75).

Q. What Brookline country club was one of the original three members of the United States Golf Association?

A. Newport Golf Club.

Q. Boston University is in what football conference?

A. Yankee.

Q. What nineteenth-century New England game involved a ball, a stick, and bases run clockwise?

A. Rounders.

Q. In what professional sport was Mike Flanagan voted Most Valuable Player in 1978?

A. Soccer.

———◆———

Q. What parts of the body can be used to propel the ball in volleyball?

A. Anything above the waist.

———◆———

Q. What round sporting ball weighs approximately 600 to 650 grams?

A. Basketball.

———◆———

Q. In 1876, the first major league baseball game to require extra innings was played by what two New England teams?

A. Hartford Blues and Boston Red Caps.

———◆———

Q. What New England game is also called New Market or Yankee Grab?

A. Going to Boston.

———◆———

Q. In 1936, what football team won the NFL East?

A. Boston Redskins.

———◆———

Q. Against what college team did Harvard play in the first football game held in Harvard Stadium?

A. Dartmouth.

Q. What three states does the 119-mile-long Americana Trail cover?

A. Connecticut, Rhode Island, and Massachusetts.

———◆———

Q. What two Bruins players took the Ross Trophy home during the 1970s?

A. Phil Esposito and Bobby Orr.

———◆———

Q. What was the name of Caroline Kennedy's pony?

A. Macaroni.

———◆———

Q. What ingredients are in the cocktail called Cape Codder?

A. Vodka and cranberry juice.

———◆———

Q. What Boston-brewed beer is named after a famous colonial patriot?

A. Samuel Adams.

———◆———

Q. What ale did President Reagan drink in 1983 at the Erie Pub in the Boston area?

A. Ballantine.

———◆———

Q. What did Mayor Ray Flynn clutch in his hands while running the Boston Marathon in 1984?

A. Rosary beads.

Q. What beer company sponsors Concerts on the Common in Boston?

A. Miller.

———◆———

Q. What New England family owns the *Marlin*, a 52-foot cabin cruiser?

A. The Kennedy family.

———◆———

Q. According to reports, in 1916, Lawrence Woodman of Essex first cooked clams in what fashion?

A. He fried them.

———◆———

Q. What team did the Patriots lose to in the 1978 playoffs?

A. Houston.

———◆———

Q. What brand of golf balls are made in New Bedford?

A. Titleist.

———◆———

Q. What Celtics player did a McChicken commercial for McDonalds?

A. Larry Bird.

———◆———

Q. In how many Stanley Cup finals were the Boston Bruins during the 70s?

A. Five.

Q. What game manufacturing company is located in Salem?

A. Parker Brothers.

———◆———

Q. What New England college claims to have been the first to use the spitball in baseball?

A. Harvard.

———◆———

Q. What toy—the largest of its type ever built—was built in Winchendon?

A. Wooden rocking horse.

———◆———

Q. What was the alleged reason the defending champ collapsed during the 1901 Boston Marathon?

A. A spectator passed him a chloroform-laced sponge.

———◆———

Q. How was the Massachusetts Snuff Mill first used?

A. As a sawmill.

———◆———

Q. Of what material are the swans at the rear of the swan boats in Boston Public Gardens made?

A. Metal.

———◆———

Q. What is the minimum sentence for carrying an unlicensed firearm in Massachusetts?

A. One-year compulsory jail.

Q. What is the maximum number of consecutive days that a camper can stay at the state-operated parks in Massachusetts?

A. Fourteen.

———◆———

Q. In what two consecutive years was John Smith the leading scorer in the AFL?

A. 1979–80.

———◆———

Q. Who shut down Cape Cod's first nude beach, situated between Truro and Wellfleet?

A. The National Park Service.

———◆———

Q. Who won the Connecticut Smythe Trophy in the 1970 and 1972 playoffs?

A. Bobby Orr.

———◆———

Q. In what conference and division do the Boston Bruins play?

A. Wales Conference, Adams Division.

———◆———

Q. What team that defeated the Bruins in the 1985–86 season went on to win the finals?

A. Montreal.

———◆———

Q. Who coached the 1939 Stanley Cup Boston hockey team?

A. Art Ross.

Q. In 1932, Dale Alexander played with what two teams while winning the American League Batting Championship?

A. Detroit and Boston.

———◆———

Q. How many years did Patriot coach Raymond Berry play for the NFL?

A. Thirteen years.

———◆———

Q. How many passes did Raymond Berry catch during his NFL career?

A. 631.

———◆———

Q. In what conference does Boston College play basketball?

A. Big East.

———◆———

Q. What Massachusetts college basketball teams play in the North Atlantic League?

A. Northeastern and Boston University.

———◆———

Q. Whom did the Celtics defeat during the NBA championship in 1986?

A. Houston.

———◆———

Q. Who tied Geoff Petrie of Portland for the NBA Rookie of the Year in 1971?

A. Dave Cowens.

Q. What Celtic great is ranked next after Wilt Chamberlain with a lifetime 21,620 rebounds?

A. Bill Russell.

Q. What Patriot won the Bert Bell Memorial Trophy in 1971?

A. Jim Plunkett.

Q. How many times did Bill Russell win the NBA Most Valuable Player award?

A. Five.

Q. How many assists did Bob Cousy have?

A. 6,955.

Q. What is the address of the Red Sox main office?

A. 24 Yawkey Way, Boston.

Q. What city, other than Boston, hosts Celtic home games?

A. Hartford, Connecticut.

Q. Whom did Harvard beat in their only Rose Bowl appearance in 1920?

A. Oregon.

Q. In what category have Jack Jensen, Dick Stuart, and Jim Rice led the American League?

A. Runs Batted In.

———◆———

Q. In 1941, Boston College beat Tennessee in what famous bowl game?

A. Sugar Bowl.

———◆———

Q. What two years did Boston College go to the Cotton Bowl?

A. 1940 and 1985.

———◆———

Q. What tool did Bob Stanley use to crush beach balls near the Red Sox bull pen?

A. A rake.

———◆———

Q. What is the nickname of the Boston University football team?

A. Terriers.

———◆———

Q. In 1985, what Patriot tied with Howie Long for the George Halas Trophy for the Best Defensive Football Player?

A. Andre Tippett.

———◆———

Q. What are the team colors for the Holy Cross Crusaders?

A. Royal blue/purple.

Q. What school hosts the Minutemen?

A. University of Massachusetts.

———◆———

Q. In 1936, what Harvard coach was selected Coach of the Year by the AFCA?

A. Dick Harlow.

———◆———

Q. What Boston College player won the Outland Award in 1985?

A. Mike Ruth.

———◆———

Q. What "first-round pick" did the Patriots receive in 1986?

A. Reggie Dupard.

———◆———

Q. How many times did Jimmy Foxx win baseball's Most Valuable Player award?

A. Three.

———◆———

Q. To how many NBA championships did Red Auerbach coach the Celtics?

A. Nine.

———◆———

Q. What Celtic forward, born in 1940, had over 26,000 NBA points?

A. John Havlicek.

Q. What Bruin led the NHL twice in scoring and five times in assists?

A. Bobby Orr.

Q. What was the final score in the 1946 Baseball All-Star game held in Boston?

A. American 12–National 0.

Q. What Bruin was "First-Team All-Star" seven times?

A. Eddie Shore.

Q. What are the two smallest baseball stadiums in the major leagues?

A. Fenway Park and Wrigley Field.

Q. What kind of license is needed to fly an ultralight in Massachusetts?

A. None.

Q. What Boston Building will house the New England Sports Museum?

A. The Customs House.

Q. What city hosts the "Tipoff Classic"?

A. Springfield.

Q. Where is the "Teddy Bear Rally" held each August?

A. Amherst.

————◆————

Q. What ski mountain is in Hancock?

A. Jiminy Peak.

SCIENCE & NATURE

C H A P T E R   S I X

Q. What national organization is responsible for the southernmost six miles of Plum Island?

A. Parker River National Wildlife Refuge.

Q. In 1955, 18 inches of rain fell on Massachusetts in what period of time?

A. 24 hours.

Q. What park in Boston contains the world's largest collection of trees and shrubs?

A. Arnold Arboretum.

Q. Who operates the McLaughlin Fish Hatchery, the largest fish hatchery east of the Mississippi River?

A. Massachusetts Division of Fisheries and Game.

Q. Quincy used to be known for what type of rock, which was used to build Bunker Hill Monument?

A. Granite.

Q. Who runs the Wellfleet Bay Wildlife Sanctuary?

A. Massachusetts Audubon Society.

———◆———

Q. What kind of whale is the Massachusetts state marine mammal?

A. The Right whale.

———◆———

Q. What killed 90 people in Worcester and vicinity on June 9, 1953?

A. A tornado.

———◆———

Q. How many days each year can bear be hunted in Massachusetts?

A. Five.

———◆———

Q. The best grouse hunting in Massachusetts can be found in what mountains?

A. The Berkshires.

———◆———

Q. What town has been the center of the Massachusetts fishing industry for generations?

A. Gloucester.

———◆———

Q. What is the average wind speed in Boston?

A. 12 miles per hour.

Q. What large thumblike shoal runs from Nantucket north to Nova Scotia?

A. Georges Bank.

———◆———

Q. Massachusetts-born Clifford Milburn Holland engineered the Holland Tunnel that passes under what river?

A. The Hudson.

———◆———

Q. What two types of fish are caught most often on the beaches on Cape Cod Bay?

A. Bluefish and stripers.

———◆———

Q. As of 1988, how many hazardous waste sites were in Massachusetts?

A. 21.

———◆———

Q. What bird did Benjamin Franklin want to be the symbol of America?

A. The turkey.

———◆———

Q. What fish found in streams on Cape Code is called a "salter"?

A. Sea-run trout.

———◆———

Q. In what language are the trees and shrubs labeled in the Arnold Arboretum?

A. Latin.

Q. What tree in the Wachusett Meadow Wildlife Sanctuary is the third largest of its kind in North America?

A. The Crocker maple.

———◆———

Q. Why did the Massachusetts State Lobster Hatchery develop the mutant blue lobster?

A. To chart migration patterns.

———◆———

Q. The April festival held on Nantucket Island honors the blooming of what flower?

A. The daffodil.

———◆———

Q. Who runs the Woods Hole Aquarium on Cape Cod?

A. National Marine Fisheries Service.

———◆———

Q. How many acres make up the Cape Cod National Seashore?

A. 27,000.

———◆———

Q. What kind of clams are usually found on Cape Cod beaches?

A. Littlenecks.

———◆———

Q. Cuttyhunk is an island in what group of Massachusetts islands?

A. Elizabeth Islands.

Q. Where is the water warmer, along Cape Cod Bay or on the Atlantic side of the Cape?

A. Bay beaches are warmer.

Q. What color are the Gay Head Cliffs on Martha's Vineyard?

A. Red.

Q. What detached Esther's Island from Nantucket in 1961?

A. A hurricane.

Q. What kind of license is needed to surfcast on Cape Cod?

A. None.

Q. What kind of fish did Louis Sirard make a record 250-pound catch off Gloucester in 1981?

A. Atlantic halibut.

Q. What mammal was brought to Nantucket Island to replace the red fox during hunts?

A. The jack rabbit.

Q. In New England, what ranking does Massachusetts have in terms of percentage of total forested land?

A. Lowest.

Q. What society runs Macomber Farm in Framingham and teaches people how to treat animals properly?

A. The Massachusetts Society for the Prevention of Cruelty to Animals.

Q. What oceanographic institute was founded in 1930 by the Rockefeller Foundation?

A. Woods Hole.

Q. What do Nantucket residents use on Ground-hog Day to determine the length of winter?

A. Quaghogs.

Q. How many miles of the Appalachian Trail pass through Massachusetts?

A. 83.

Q. What type of seafood made Ipswich famous?

A. Ipswich clams.

Q. What kind of scallops are found in shallow water around Cape Cod?

A. Bay scallops.

Q. Tewksbury is known as the world capital of what flower?

A. Carnation.

Q. What crop thrives in the southeastern coastal area of Massachusetts?

A. Cranberries.

◆

Q. What submarine sank during a test dive 220 miles east of Boston?

A. USS *Thresher*.

◆

Q. What color were Gillette's early blades?

A. Blue.

◆

Q. What type of vehicle was the "Indian," made in Springfield in 1905?

A. Motorcycle.

◆

Q. Where is Marconi Station, the first trans-Atlantic radio on the U.S. mainland?

A. Cape Cod.

◆

Q. Why are dense, low-growing plants used for displays in Boston's parks?

A. To survive the winds.

◆

Q. The Massachusetts state dog is a crossbreed of what two animals?

A. English Bulldog and English Terrier.

Q. What Dalton company produces the paper for the nation's currency?

A. Crane and Company.

———◆———

Q. What type of drawbridge is the Cape Cod Canal bridge?

A. Vertical lift.

———◆———

Q. What company produces 85 percent of all the cranberry products in North America?

A. Ocean Spray Cranberries, Inc.

———◆———

Q. In what town did the first elephant in America arrive and walk down Pickering Wharf?

A. Salem.

———◆———

Q. To what retailer did Polaroid first sell their 60-second Land Camera?

A. Jordan Marsh Company.

———◆———

Q. What is the Welch Cob, which is bred at the Grazing Fields Farm in Buzzards Bay?

A. A stocky short-legged horse.

———◆———

Q. What type of fog signal was first erected on Boston Light?

A. A cannon.

Q. What was the first atomic-powered steam electric plant in New England?

A. Yankee Atomic Electric Company.

———◆———

Q. In 1978, what destroyed the parking lot at Cape Cod's National Seashore in Eastham?

A. A blizzard.

———◆———

Q. At a Chicopee festival, what type of food was 25 feet, 4 inches long, and weighed 236 pounds?

A. Kielbasa.

———◆———

Q. Where in Boston can visitors see the colors of a human voice, be shocked, and visit distant galaxies?

A. Boston Museum of Science.

———◆———

Q. What Boston suburb contained America's first successful iron works company?

A. Saugus.

———◆———

Q. What month are flounder at their peak in Boston Harbor?

A. October.

———◆———

Q. What Boston-based company does continuous research on shaving technology?

A. Gillette.

Q. What great animal trainer is buried in Charlton's Bay Path Cemetery?

A. Grizzly Adams.

Q. In 1969, what ship experienced hull failure off the Massachusetts coast, causing an 8.8-million gallon oil spill?

A. The KEO.

Q. What famous printer and scientist signed the Declaration of Independence and the Peace Treaty with Britain?

A. Benjamin Franklin.

Q. In 1846, Dr. William Morton published the results he obtained while using ether during surgery at what hospital?

A. Massachusetts General (Boston).

Q. What religious group invented wrinkleproof and water-repellent cloth?

A. The Shakers.

Q. The first lighting of a theater from a central power station was witnessed by what famous scientist in Brockton?

A. Thomas Edison.

Q. At what Boston hospital were birth control pills proved to be effective in 1959?

A. Brigham and Women's Hospital.

Q. Where was the first liquid-fueled rocket launched?

A. Auburn.

———◆———

Q. What six words were spoken by Alexander Bell in the first telephone message?

A. "Come here, Watson. I want you."

———◆———

Q. What product made from hemp sails, canvas, and rope was invented in 1843 in South Braintree?

A. Manila paper.

———◆———

Q. What gun invented by a Massachusetts native is called "the gun that won the west"?

A. The Colt revolver.

———◆———

Q. What Boston native invented the wet-suit and webbed sandals?

A. Benjamin Franklin.

———◆———

Q. Simon Willard of Massachusetts obtained a patent in 1802 for what kind of clock?

A. The "banjo" clock.

———◆———

Q. What invention did Elisha Gray believe she invented, although someone else got the credit for it?

A. The telephone.

Q. Where were the model 1795 musket rifle, 1903 rifle, M–1 rifle, and M–14 rifle developed?

A. Springfield Armory.

Q. At what New England college was the first computer developed in 1928?

A. Massachusetts Institute of Technology.

Q. What was the Franklin stove originally called by its inventor?

A. The Pennsylvania Fireplace.

Q. The wooden clothespin and the flat broom were invented by what group?

A. The Shakers.

Q. In what city did Alexander Graham Bell demonstrate the first telephone?

A. Boston.

Q. What company was founded by Linus Yale of Selburne?

A. Yale Lock Company.

Q. What kind of pencil, made of silver, black lead, calcined gypsum, and lampblack, was invented in Northampton?

A. The indelible pencil.

Q. What is the nation's third oldest engineering college?

A. Worcester Polytechnic Institute (1865).

———◆———

Q. Ellen Swallow Richards, who studied nutrition and environment, was the first woman to graduate from what college?

A. Massachusetts Institute of Technology.

———◆———

Q. What kind of tricky welding did the early Massachusetts blacksmith practice?

A. Fire welding (open flame).

———◆———

Q. What is the common name for *Adalia bipuctata*, the state insect of New Hampshire and Massachusetts?

A. Ladybug.

———◆———

Q. About how many miles can the Woods Hole research vehicle *Alvin* be submerged?

A. Two.

———◆———

Q. What Massachusetts swamp plant can be used as a vegetable, pancake flour, potato substitute, or just eaten raw?

A. Cattail.

———◆———

Q. What is the Massachusetts state animal?

A. The Morgan horse.

Q. What would many large companies like to search for under the Georges Bank off the Massachusetts coast?

A. Oil.

———◆———

Q. In Massachusetts native Samuel Morse's telegraph code, what letter of the alphabet is the "shortest"?

A. E (one dot).

———◆———

Q. What test does Ocean Spray use to find the cranberries of the highest quality?

A. Bounce one seven times.

———◆———

Q. What is the best way to tell if a substance is scrimshaw or plastic?

A. Plastic melts.

———◆———

Q. What are *Fucus* and *Ascophyllum,* found off the Massachusetts coast?

A. Seaweed.

———◆———

Q. What reptiles are the most numerous in Massachusetts?

A. Snakes.

———◆———

Q. Found in moist places throughout Massachusetts, what color algae is Irish moss?

A. Red.

Q. What do all iris roots found in Massachusetts have in common?

A. They are all poisonous.

———◆———

Q. The cranberry is richest in what vitamin?

A. C.

———◆———

Q. How many years does it take from the installation and planting of a cranberry bog until the first harvest?

A. Five.

———◆———

Q. The fish that is called an *alewife* in Maine and a *buckeye* in Rhode Island is called what in Massachusetts?

A. Herring.

———◆———

Q. Of bee stings, snake bites, or spider bites, which kill more people in Massachusetts each year?

A. Bee stings.

———◆———

Q. What "bank" produces more food fish per acre than almost anywhere in the world?

A. Georges Bank.

———◆———

Q. The blue flag wildflower found near wet places in Massachusetts is a member of what family?

A. The Iris family.

Q. When is the Massachusetts strawberry season?

A. Mid- to-late June.

———◆———

Q. Where do Massachusetts herons nest?

A. In trees.

———◆———

Q. What is the largest meat-eating animal found in Massachusetts?

A. The black bear.

———◆———

Q. What Massachusetts plant is called "ragged sailor"?

A. Chicory.

———◆———

Q. What did the "Nantucket sleigh ride" mean to a whaler?

A. A boat being pulled by a harpooned whale.

———◆———

Q. What disease is endangering the American elm trees in Massachusetts?

A. Dutch Elm disease.

———◆———

Q. What are the only three native American fruits found in Massachusetts?

A. Cranberry, blueberry, and Concord grape.

SCIENCE & NATURE

Q. What is the state bird?

A. Chickadee.

———◆———

Q. What is the largest member of the squirrel family found in Massachusetts?

A. The woodchuck.

———◆———

Q. What is the approximate weight of Plymouth Rock?

A. Six tons.

———◆———

Q. What is the Massachusetts state tree?

A. American elm.

———◆———

Q. Where is the Pratt Geology Museum?

A. Amherst College.

———◆———

Q. At what Andover Academy is the Robert S. Peabody Foundation for Archaeology?

A. Phillips.

———◆———

Q. At 3,491 feet, what is the highest peak in the state?

A. Mt. Greylock.

SCIENCE & NATURE

Q. Where is the Computer Museum?

A. Museum Wharf, Boston.

———◆———

Q. What Boston building houses the restored laboratory where Alexander Graham Bell spoke the first words heard through a telephone?

A. The New England Telephone Building.

———◆———

Q. Where is the largest cylindrical saltwater tank stocked with over 600 species?

A. New England Aquarium, Boston.

———◆———

Q. The Arnold Arboretum contains how many varieties of trees and shrubs?

A. Over 7,000.

———◆———

Q. How many bird species frequent the Great Meadows Wildlife Refuge near Concord?

A. 214.

———◆———

Q. In Dennis, who developed the commercial growing of cranberries?

A. Henry Hall.

———◆———

Q. Where can one trace the growth of maritime steam power?

A. Marine Museum, Fall River.

SCIENCE & NATURE

Q. What Falmouth facility researches new ways of providing food, energy and shelter?

A. The New Alchemy Institute.

———◆———

Q. What botanical garden and sanctuary of the New England Wild Flower Society is in Framingham?

A. The Garden in the Woods.

———◆———

Q. Where is the Albert Schweitzer Center?

A. Great Barrington.

———◆———

Q. Where is the Granby Dinosaur Museum?

A. Holyoke.

———◆———

Q. Pleasant Valley Wildlife Sanctuary is near what town?

A. Lenox.

———◆———

Q. What town is the birthplace of Maria Mitchell, America's first woman astronomer?

A. Nantucket.

———◆———

Q. What 55-million-year-old rock formation in North Adams was popularized by Nathaniel Hawthorne?

A. Natural Bridge.

Q. What city had a trans-Atlantic cable station that provided direct communication to Brest, France, from 1897 to 1959?

A. Orleans.

Q. What town is the location of General Electric's main transformer plant?

A. Pittsfield.

Q. What town is called the "birthplace of the American steel industry"?

A. Saugus.

Q. Where is the Bridge of Flowers?

A. Shelburne Falls.

Q. What river was dammed in the 1930s to create the Quabbin Reservoir?

A. Swift.

Q. Where is the Babson World Globe and Map of the United States?

A. Wellesley.

Q. In the 1840s, what medical disorder did Oliver Wendell Holmes research?

A. Childbed fever.

Q. When did William Morton perform the first appendectomy?

A. 1886.

———◆———

Q. When did Massachusetts establish the first state board of health in the nation?

A. 1869.

———◆———

Q. With what substance did Indians line their iron kettles so that they would not taste the iron?

A. Clay.

———◆———

Q. The Pilgrims thought cranberry blossoms resembled the head of what bird?

A. The crane.

———◆———

Q. By what name was the famous nurseryman and missionary John Chapman better known?

A. Johnny Appleseed.

———◆———

Q. In 1737, plant-lover Andrew Faneuil built what structure that was the first of its kind in Boston?

A. A greenhouse.

———◆———

Q. Sailors ate cranberries to ward off what ailment?

A. Scurvy.

Q. For what purpose did the early settlers use the fruit from the bayberry shrub?

A. Fragrant bayberry candles.

Q. Who spoke the first telephone message to Thomas Augustus Watson?

A. Alexander Graham Bell.

Q. Dr. Daniel Fisher, once the richest man on Martha's Vineyard, had a contract to supply all lighthouses with what commodity?

A. Whale oil.

Q. How far does Cape Ann extend into the sea?

A. 12 miles.

Q. What Harvard instructor, designer of the Mark I computer, said there would never be a need for more than one or two computers in the world?

A. Howard H. Aiken.

Q. What university is both a land grant and sea grant institution?

A. Massachusetts Institute of Technology.

Q. What Gloucester native founded three colleges and established in New Hampshire a center for the study of gravity?

A. Roger W. Babson.

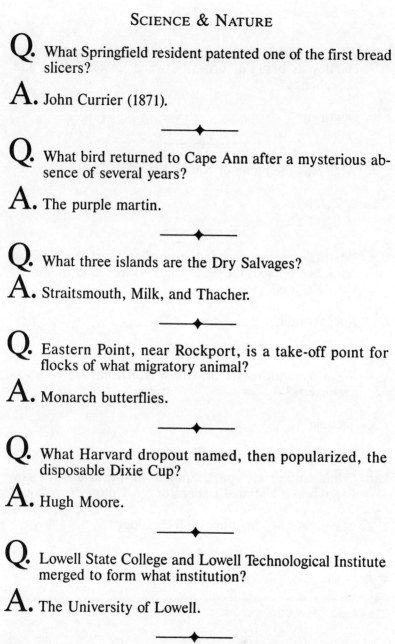

Q. What Springfield resident patented one of the first bread slicers?

A. John Currier (1871).

Q. What bird returned to Cape Ann after a mysterious absence of several years?

A. The purple martin.

Q. What three islands are the Dry Salvages?

A. Straitsmouth, Milk, and Thacher.

Q. Eastern Point, near Rockport, is a take-off point for flocks of what migratory animal?

A. Monarch butterflies.

Q. What Harvard dropout named, then popularized, the disposable Dixie Cup?

A. Hugh Moore.

Q. Lowell State College and Lowell Technological Institute merged to form what institution?

A. The University of Lowell.

Q. What were the three peak years for sea serpent sightings in Gloucester Harbor?

A. 1817 through 1819.

SCIENCE & NATURE

Q. What area of deserted moors was described by Marsden Hartley as being a "cross between Easter Island and Stonehenge"?

A. Dogtown.

Q. What was the name of Nantucket's first ferry?

A. *Telegraph.*

Q. What Gloucester park is the northernmost reach of the *Magnolia glauca*, the only magnolia tree to grow wild in New England?

A. Ravenswood.

Q. What mountains lie on the western border of Massachusetts?

A. Taconic.

Q. What university participates in programs at the Brookhaven National Laboratory in Upton, New York?

A. Massachusetts Institute of Technology.

Q. What bird is named for a Cape Ann town?

A. The Ipswich sparrow.

Q. Triassic-age sandstone is responsible for the reddish brown soil of what fertile valley?

A. Connecticut River Valley.

Q. What Cape Ann cove was named for a bird that was once abundant but is now extinct?

A. Pigeon Cove (for the passenger pigeons).

———◆———

Q. What was the name of the conservation campaign that prevented a long stretch of marshland along Route 128 from being commercially developed?

A. "A Window on the Marsh."

———◆———

Q. What Gloucester inventor's extensive experiments with remote controlled vehicles set the stage for the exploration of space?

A. John Hays Hammond, Jr.

———◆———

Q. Before experimenting with frozen foods, what job did Clarence Birdseye hold?

A. Field naturalist for the United States Biological Survey.

———◆———

Q. What MIT graduate made a national reputation by predicting the 1929 crash of the stock market?

A. Roger W. Babson.

———◆———

Q. What hospital has treated so many musicians for finger problems that it has announced an unusual specialty nicknamed "musical medicine"?

A. Massachusetts General.

———◆———

Q. What apprentice to a Boston watchmaker invented the sewing machine?

A. Elias Howe.

Q. In what city were the first mass-produced watches made?

A. Waltham.

Q. What Belmont stables housed the first Holstein cattle brought into the United States?

A. Chenery.

Q. With what type of device was Alexander Graham Bell experimenting when he invented the telephone?

A. Electrical hearing aids.

Q. What Lynnfield "Bean Man" is dedicated to preserving America's heirloom beans?

A. John E. Withee.

Q. What Polish immigrant founded the New England Hospital for Women and Children?

A. Marie Zakrzewska.

Q. What Springfield brothers were the first to successfully operate an American-made automobile (September 1893)?

A. Charles and Frank Duryea.

Q. What invention of William Howe made the construction of railroad bridges more efficient and cost effective?

A. The Howe truss.

Q. U.S. patent No. 1,647 for "Telegraph Signs" was granted to what Charlestown native?

A. Samuel F. B. Morse.

———◆———

Q. What Peabody company patented a two-way picture telephone system?

A. PicTel Corporation.

———◆———

Q. When he invented the liquid-fueled rocket, Robert Goddard was chairman of the physics department at what university?

A. Clark (in Worcester).

———◆———

Q. What early advocate of using wheat flour that retained the bran was called the "poet of bran" by Ralph Waldo Emerson?

A. Rev. Sylvester Graham.

———◆———

Q. What did Milton-born R. Buckminster Fuller call his idea for creating a device that derived the maximum output from minimum material and energy?

A. The Dymaxion principle.

———◆———

Q. What Stockbridge native laid the first trans-Atlantic cable?

A. Cyrus Field.

———◆———

Q. What Harvard professor invented the iron lung?

A. Dr. Philip Drinker.

Q. New Bedford-born Hetty Green inherited $5 million, but became such a miser that she was known by what nickname?

A. The Witch of Wall Street.

Q. What did Earl Tupper, who formed the Tupperware Corporation in Farnumsville, call the material that he used to make everything from poker chips to ice cube trays?

A. Poly T.

Q. While living in Worcester, Joshua Stoddard realized his dream of using steam to make music by inventing what instrument?

A. Calliope.

Q. To what Roxbury native did the Smithsonian Institution originally give credit for inventing the first airplane capable of manned flight, denying the Wright brothers' claim for several decades?

A. Samuel P. Langley.

Q. What stream is the Connecticut River's largest tributary?

A. Chicopee.

Q. In 1858 what Boston detective invented the first practical electronic burglar alarm?

A. E. T. Holmes.

Q. What Lynn native created a vegetable compound described as the "Weary Woman's Sure Friend"?

A. Lydia E. Pinkham.

Q. How many ships wrecked in the waters off Nantucket Island between 1843 and 1903?

A. More than 2,100.

———◆———

Q. Who led the Massachusetts General Hospital team to Antarctica's McMurdo Sound to discover why seals do not get the bends?

A. Warren Zapol.

———◆———

Q. In 1875 a narrow gauge railroad was built connecting Boston with what natural resort area?

A. Revere Beach.

———◆———

Q. In what Massachusetts Institute of Technology building is research into solar energy conducted?

A. Solar Building 5.

———◆———

Q. What two Harvard physicists shared the 1979 Nobel Prize for Physics with Abdus Salam of London's Imperial College?

A. Sheldon Glashow and Steven Weinberg.

———◆———

Q. What musical organization is made up of members of a noted scientific community?

A. Woods Hole Cantata Consort.

———◆———

Q. What Westboro resident is known for creating more than 75 varieties of irises and chronicling her work in *The World of Irises*?

A. Beatrice Warburton.

Q. What percentage of Massachusetts' drinking water is supplied by the Quabbin Reservoir?

A. 40 percent.

———◆———

Q. Approximately how many mill dams exist in Massachusetts, although only a handful do any useful work?

A. 6,000.

———◆———

Q. What small-town-produced paper was judged at the 1853 World's Fair to be the finest in the world?

A. Tyringham Bond.

———◆———

Q. What Tyringham artist's "ultimate studio" is one of the finest examples of individualized architecture in the world?

A. Sir Henry Kitson.

———◆———

Q. What inventor, known as the "Nutshell Man," made his home in the Chesterfield Gorge?

A. Chandler Clarence Clayton Bicknell.

———◆———

Q. What railroad tunnel in the Berkshires region, built between 1851 and 1875, is still in use and often visited by many railroad buffs?

A. Hoosac.

———◆———

Q. What town's industry changed from wool production to cattle farming following two disatrous floods that wiped out the factories?

A. Middlefield.

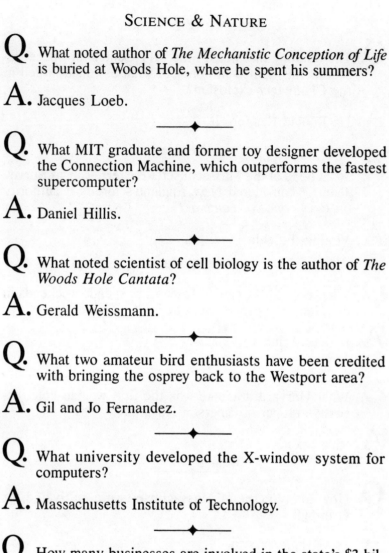

Q. What noted author of *The Mechanistic Conception of Life* is buried at Woods Hole, where he spent his summers?

A. Jacques Loeb.

———◆———

Q. What MIT graduate and former toy designer developed the Connection Machine, which outperforms the fastest supercomputer?

A. Daniel Hillis.

———◆———

Q. What noted scientist of cell biology is the author of *The Woods Hole Cantata*?

A. Gerald Weissmann.

———◆———

Q. What two amateur bird enthusiasts have been credited with bringing the osprey back to the Westport area?

A. Gil and Jo Fernandez.

———◆———

Q. What university developed the X-window system for computers?

A. Massachusetts Institute of Technology.

———◆———

Q. How many businesses are involved in the state's $3 billion food processing industry?

A. More than 600.

———◆———

Q. What former high school teacher's archaeological research turned up the pirate ship *Whydah*, which had sunk off Cape Cod carrying $400 million in gold and silver?

A. Barry Clifford.

Q. The building that houses the MIT Center for Space Research was named in honor of what astronaut killed in the *Challenger* explosion?

A. Dr. Ronald E. McNair.

Q. What head of the Massachusetts Eastern Cougar Survey Team is considered New England's foremost authority on *Felis concolor couguar*?

A. Virginia Fifield.

Q. What noted MIT cancer researcher spends weekends in the New Hampshire cabin he built by hand?

A. Robert Weinberg.

Q. What Harvard graduate was the first woman chief executive officer of Emerson Hospital?

A. Rina Spence.

Q. How many acres of Massachusetts are cultivated for farming?

A. More than 600,000.